LIABILITY AND SAFETY
IN PHYSICAL EDUCATION
AND SPORT

A practitioner's guide to the legal
aspects of teaching and coaching
in elementary and secondary schools

James E. Hart
and
Robert J. Ritson

National Association for Sport and Physical Education
an association of the
American Alliance for Health, Physical Education,
Recreation and Dance

The American Alliance for Health, Physical Education, Recreation and Dance is an educational organization designed to support, encourage, and provide assistance to member groups and their personnel nationwide as they initiate, develop, and conduct programs in health, leisure, and movement-related activities. The Alliance seeks to:

- Encourage, guide, and support professional growth and development in health, leisure, and movement-related programs based on individual needs, interests, and capabilities.
- Communicate the importance of health, leisure, and movement-related activities as they contribute to human well-being.
- Encourage and facilitate research which will enrich health, leisure, and movement-related activities and to disseminate the findings to professionals and the public.
- Develop and evaluate standards and guidelines for personnel and programs in health, leisure, and movement-related activities.
- Coordinate and administer a planned program of professional, public, and government relations that will improve education in areas of health, leisure, and movement-related activities.
- Conduct other activities for the public benefit.

TABLE OF CONTENTS

APPENDIXES

About the Authors

James E. Hart, EdD and Robert J. Ritson, PhD bring together a blend of background experiences that combine to produce practical insight into the day to day issues of liability and safety encountered by physical educators, coaches, and program administrators in the elementary and secondary school settings.

Hart currently teaches physical education and serves as athletic director at Kelly Middle School in Eugene, Oregon. He also coaches cross country and track and field at neighboring North Eugene High School. He has 21 years of public school experience, including 10 years as an elementary school physical education specialist and 11 years as a middle school physical educator. He has been active in curriculum development and spent two years on a special assignment for curriculum development and implementation in the Eugene School District.

Ritson is the physical education curriculum coordinator with the Oregon State Department of Education. He spent five years as a public school physical education specialist followed by 10 years at the University of Oregon and one year at Boise State University. He contributes to the professional preparation program in teacher education and serves as a liaison between the university and local school districts and staff on projects geared toward the improvement of educational experiences for children.

Both Hart and Ritson have conducted workshops on a variety of topics at the local, state, and national levels. Both have a strong commitment to professional associations in physical education and have served in leadership positions. Through their combined experiences, they have had the opportunity to share and interact with professional practitioners in elementary and secondary school physical education nationwide. Their understanding and appreciation for the issues and challenges that face teachers, coaches, and administrators on a daily basis is reflected in their presentation of this volume on liability and sport issues.

Preface

Professionals involved in physical education and coaching must continually strive to provide the safest environment and leadership in delivering programs. These professionals are often resources to other educators who are conducting co-curricular and extracurricular activities involving physical activity. The information in this book will offer guidance for safer programs and management of risk while reinforcing sound educational practice.

The book provides concise, readable introductions to the concepts of the law and presents practical examples of situations from the "trenches." Case studies illustrate a wide variety of teacher/coach/administrator actions, as well as environmental and equipment conditions, that have been challenged in courts across the country. The case studies focus on the practical application of the law, offering guidance for the practitioner.

Summaries of the steps physical educators and coaches can take to deliver safer programs are given at the end of each section. Labelled "The Reasonably Prudent Physical Educator or Coach ..." these lists contain practical advice concerning the issues covered in the case studies.

We believe this material will be of great assistance to K-12 educators and an excellent resource for college/university level courses on legal aspects of sport and physical eduation. It will help professionals maximize safety. The authors, who are engaged in delivering programs to students and face the day-to-day issues and challenges of physical education and sport, bring extensive knowledge and experience to these important concerns. All physical educators and coaches will benefit from reviewing their own programs and actions for compliance with the "reasonable and prudent" standard ably set forth in this book.

Judy Young
Executive Director,
National Association for
Sport and Physical Education

Introduction

Physical education and sport offer a wide variety of opportunities for the total development of school-age children and youth. Along with all other disciplines, physical education and sport help students acquire essential learning skills through common curriculum goals. As students advance through the grades, physical education and sports programs enhance the social, emotional, and intellectual growth common to the goals of other curricular areas while adding a unique emphasis on fitness, movement, skill development, group work and movement aesthetics.

In recent years we have witnessed a greater acknowledgment of the importance and an expansion of physical education and sport programs. There has been a rapid increase in elementary school programs characterized by a staff of specialists, inclusion of the handicapped in school programs, coeducation in all classes at all levels, and the increased opportunity for off-campus as well as on-campus activities. Intramural activities at both the elementary and secondary levels have become common outgrowths of the instructional program and athletic opportunities have increased, particularly in the area of girls' athletics.

The American system of public education has become very interrelated with the legal system within which it works. The last two decades have seen a dramatic increase in the influence of the legal system on the day-to-day operation of schools. The sources of this influence are many. The combination of constitutions, statutes and cases of common law form the primary legal foundation on which schools are based. Federal and state constitutions, statutory enactments such as PL 94-142 and Title IX, collective bargaining legislation, and the enormous body of judicial decisions or case law have daily impact not only on school systems themselves but on the teachers and students who make up these systems as well. The law has established criteria or standards for entering the teaching profession, established the conditions under which teachers work, and delineated teachers' rights and responsibilities as well as the rights of students.

Litigation has become a way of life in our society as the public has become quite sophisticated and willing to seek legal redress for perceived wrongs. Physical education and athletic staffs have numerous opportunities to become entangled in legal disputes. While PL 94-142 and Title IX legislation have directly affected the manner in which programs are conducted and the constitutional rights of students and athletes have come under examination, tort liability for negligence continues to be the major cause for legal action in the physical education and athletic settings. The number of litigations involving injured pupils and athletes has increased significantly in the last 20 years. This may be explained in part by the expansion of programs and the development of new facilities and equipment which have increased the opportunity for students to participate in many new and varied activities.

An injury problem clearly exists within physical education and sport. The injury problem is a function of both the large number of participants and the nature of the programs themselves. Both programs are characterized by activities which have participants actively moving and interacting physically as well as socially. They involve activities with some degree of elevated risk due to actual or possible physical contact and which may be physically challenging to the student or athlete. The magnitude of the problem is significant. *Principles of Safety in Physical Education and Sport*, a 1987 publication of the American Alliance for Health, Physical Education, Recreation and Dance, reports that in a single calendar year, 1.8 million participants between the ages of 5 and 14 received medically-attended injuries while engaged in physical education and sport programs.[1] While these injuries are classified as accidents, they are frequently the result of factors which lead predictably to injuries. As reported in *Principles of Safety in Physical Education and Sport*, these injuries can often be traced directly to social, environmental or behavioral factors which, if controlled, would result in dramatic reductions in both deaths and injuries.

While injuries are often viewed as a natural risk of participation in physical education and sport programs, it is important to not allow the social, environmental and behavioral factors involved in these injuries to go uncontrolled. It is imperative that physical educators, coaches, and administrators of these programs foresee the risks associated with the activities they offer to students and athletes and that they make every reasonable effort to reduce the risks while conducting their programs.

Because of the increased risk associated with activity programs within physical education and sport, physical educators and coaches are exposed to an increased likelihood of becoming involved in a legal incident. It is important that they have a basic working knowledge of the law as it relates to sport and physical education.

The focus of this publication is on tort liability for negligence. An overview of tort liability and negligence theory is presented, followed by a discussion of various defenses employed by school districts and their employees when engaged in a lawsuit. Finally, the duties and responsibilities of physical educators and coaches, and other allied professionals, are presented along with numerous case summaries which serve to further illustrate the duties and the standard of care to which professional physical educators and coaches are held while alerting the reader to the kinds of teacher/coach actions as well as environmental conditions which have given rise to litigation.

Each case summary has a legal reference citation for the national reporter system indicating where the case is located, if the reader wishes to refer to the actual report in a law library. The first number in the citation indicates the volume number of the reporter in which the case is located. Next is an abbreviation for the reporter name, followed by the page number on which the case begins. For example, in Larson V. Independent School District (see page 24), 289 N.W. 2d 112 means that the case may be found in Volume 289 of the North Western Reporter, second series, beginning on page 112. The various reporters are listed in the Appendix.

The case summaries presented were selected because of their practical application in day-to-day school settings. Notes are added to many of the summaries to point out their special significance or call attention to particularly important considerations.

Additional cases of interest to physical educators and coaches are listed in the appendix for those who wish to pursue further study in liability issues.

As with any profession, the law has a language of its own. While every attempt has been made to keep the text in ordinary language, the use of legal terms and phrases was unavoidable. Therefore, a glossary of terms has been included in the appendix for the convenience of the reader.

Notations to the text appear in the appendix section labeled endnotes. Materials used in the preparation of this book are listed in the references section.

James E. Hart
Robert J. Ritson

Tort Law and Negligence Theory

The "body of law which is directed toward the compensation of individuals for losses which they have suffered within the scope of their legally-recognized interests [is known] as the law of torts."[2] It serves to compensate, indemnify, prevent or penalize losses which individuals are subjected to by the activities of others. Simply stated, the primary function of the law of torts is to determine when such losses should be shifted from one individual to another and when they should be allowed to remain where they have fallen.[3]

Tort law covers three broad areas. They include intentional acts to harm, strict liability and unintentional acts which result in harm. Intentional acts to harm include actions which interfere with property; disturbances of intangible interests as is the case in libel and slander, invasion of privacy and misrepresentation, deceit and fraud; and interference with person as in assault and battery and physical or sexual abuse. Strict liability is liability without fault. "The focus of strict liability is on the dangerousness of the activity or product, rather than on the conduct or intent of a defendant.... The activities which give rise to strict liability are not so unreasonable as to be prohibited altogether, but they are sufficiently dangerous or provide unusual risks so that the law requires them to be conducted at the peril of the one sponsoring the activity."[4] Abnormally dangerous equipment or activities and product liability are subject to the standard of strict liability. Unintentional acts resulting in harm include any alleged negligent behavior. While intentional torts and strict liability occasionally surface in the physical education and athletic settings, tort liability for negligence remains as the leading cause of legal action in this area.

Negligence is the failure to act as a reasonably prudent person would act in the same or similar circumstances. Negligence theory has been established on the principle that those who are harmed by the carelessness of others should be compensated by the wrong doers.

Negligence depends upon the existence of four essential elements. To recover damages in court actions for negligence, all four elements must be present. They include:

1. A duty or obligation, recognized by law, requiring a person to conform to a certain standard of conduct for the protection of others against unreasonable risk.
2. A failure on a person's part to conform to the required standard of conduct; a breach of duty.
3. A reasonably close causal connection between the conduct and the resulting injury; proximate or legal cause.
4. Actual loss or damage; a legally-recognizable injury.

The absence of any one of these essential elements of negligence will bar recovery of damages under the law.

DUTY ISSUE

In any action seeking to recover damages as a result of negligence, the plaintiff must show that the defendant, as a matter of law, owed a duty of care to the plaintiff. Duty requires an individual to conform to a standard of conduct for the protection of others against unreasonable risks and rests upon the existence of some relationship between the parties. This rule of duty arises out of both common law and statute. As discussed by van der Smissen, this duty can originate from a relationship which is inherent in the situation or one which is voluntarily assumed or it can be a duty expressly prescribed by statute. There is no question that a duty exists on the part of physical educators, coaches, administrators and school districts to exercise reasonable care to protect students from harm.

Foreseeability is a central element in the question of duty. A duty of reasonable care in protecting others from harm is required whenever a foreseeable risk of harm exists. Courts will not assign liability where the defendant could not have reasonably foreseen the danger or risk in a given action or situation.

The standard of care required by duty is one of reasonable and ordinary care under the circumstances. What constitutes reasonable and ordinary care is unique to each specific case and varies with the facts and circumstances of a situation as they are, or should be known, to a defendant. Ordinary care in one case might very well be deemed negligence under different circumstances or surroundings.

The extent and nature of the duty owed can vary depending on the status of the individuals involved. Anyone who comes onto the school's property assumes the status of trespasser, licensee, or invitee. A trespasser is a person who enters without consent of the school or district. A licensee is an individual who enters for his/her own purposes but with the express or implied consent of the school or district. An invitee is a person who enters at the express or implied invitation of the school or district to pursue the purpose for which it is held open. The highest standard of care is owed to the invitee with the least being afforded to the trespasser.

There is generally no duty owed to trespassers. They are normally held to be responsible for their own safety although there are some limitations on this absence of duty. Generally, no duty exists except to refrain from willful, wanton, or reckless disregard for the safety of the trespasser. The law does treat some child trespassers differently. Under the attractive nuisance doctrine, child trespassers are afforded ordinary care against foreseeable risks. A short discussion relative to the attractive nuisance doctrine is included later in the section on equipment, grounds, and facilities.

The duty owed to a licensee consists of warning them of dangerous natural and artificial conditions on the premises of which the school or district has actual knowledge. There is no duty to inspect the premises for such conditions.

A duty of reasonable care in avoiding the causing of an injury to the licensee is required of all school personnel while conducting their own activities. The invitee, on the other hand, is present at the express or implied invitation of the school or district, and the district has the duty to inspect and discover dangerous conditions and activities on the premises. Depending on the danger involved, the school or district must either warn the invitee or make the condition or activity safe. Students, parents, playground users, and outside groups using the school facilities through community school programs are classified as invitees.

Duty arises only under affirmative conduct, the exception being where a "special" relationship exists. Duty and the standard of care are extended under special relationships, holding a person liable not only for their acts but their omissions as well. Teachers and coaches are part of a special relationship along with students and as a result, the standard of care is increased. Because of the student-teacher relationship, the law not only compels teachers and coaches to use reasonable care in conducting their activities, but in a number of cases imposes a duty to perform certain tasks. Special training as educators and coaches also serves to extend the duty or standard of care required beyond that of a reasonable and prudent person. As noted by Morris, if an individual has chosen to engage in an activity requiring special skills, education, training, or experience, then the standard by which his/her conduct is measured is that of the reasonably skilled, competent and experienced person who is a qualified member of the group authorized to engage in that activity.[5]

The responsibilities of physical educators and athletic staff under their duty of care are set forth by common law and statute. They include adequate and proper instruction; supervision; inspetion of facilities, grounds, and equipment; rendering first aid; and safe transportation. Specific responsibilities under each of these broad categories are numerous; they are detailed in the section on "Duties of Physical Education and Sport Staff and Supporting Case Law."

BREACH OF DUTY ISSUE

Breach of duty constitutes unreasonable conduct and may be the outcome of either malfeasance, misfeasance or nonfeasance. Malfeasance is the performance of an improper or illegal act, misfeasance is the improper performance of a legal act and nonfeasance is the failure to act where obligated to do so. While anyone can be guilty of malfeasance and misfeasance, nonfeasance requires the existence of a special relationship between the parties, such as in the case of teacher and student. Most negligence actions are based on affirmative conduct judged to be unreasonable or misfeasance. In all cases, negligence requires the breach of a legal duty, not merely a moral or humane duty.

The "standard of care" is the measure by which the actions of individuals are gauged in court actions for negligence. Courts have held that an individual is required to exercise that degree of care and foresight which a reasonably prudent person would exercise under the same or similar circumstances. A synthesis of common law allows the conclusion that the degree of care required is ordinary and reasonable care.

The rule of ordinary care prevails at all times, but what constitutes ordinary care can vary depending upon the circumstances. Factors such as the age and capacity of the participants, type of activity and environmental conditions are considered when deciding what constitutes ordinary care under the circumstances.

In evaluating the breach of duty issue, courts will be asking whether, given a particular set of circumstances, the reasonably prudent person should have been able to recognize and foresee an unreasonable risk or likelihood of harm to others. Once again, because of the special training, skills and experience of teachers and coaches, their actions will be measured against the standard of a reasonably skilled, competent and experienced teacher or coach who is qualified and authorized to conduct physical education and sport programs.

The courts, in deciding what a reasonably prudent person would have done in a given set of circumstances, apply a balancing test. Simply stated, if the risk of harm outweighs the inconvenience of taking precautions to avoid injury, the reasonable person would take the precautions. On the other hand, if the risk of harm is slight compared to the relatively high burden or inconvenience of the precautions, the reasonable person would proceed without the precautions. Standards employed in the teaching and coaching field which are endorsed by professional organizations and supported by current professional literature will be used as one measure in determining whether an individual teacher's or coach's actions satisfy the reasonable and prudent standard.

CAUSAL RELATION ISSUE

Liability for negligence cannot be assigned by the court unless it can be shown that a causal connection exists between the alleged negligent action and the injury sustained by the plaintiff. Causal relation is a neutral issue, unaffected by the right or wrong of an individual's conduct. While philosophical, scientific and moral evaluations of a defendant's conduct are relevant in examining the issues of duty, breach of duty and damage, they are irrelevant to the issue of causal relation. The court makes no attempt to ascertain all the causes or *the* cause and it makes no attempt to determine why the defendant acted the way he or she did. When dealing with causal relation, the only issue of interest is the defendant's contribution to the plaintiff's injury.

The legal cause, recognized by the court as the connection between the action and resulting injury, is often referred to as the proximate cause. *Black's Law Dictionary* defines proximate cause as "that which, in a natural and continuous sequence, unbroken by an efficient intervening cause, produces injury and without which the result would not have occurred." Intervening cause "is an independent cause which intervenes between the original wrongful act or omission and the injury, turns aside the natural sequence of events, and produces a result which would not otherwise have followed and which could not have been reasonably anticipated."[6] In other words, if there is an intervening cause which produces an unforeseeable injury, the person guilty of the original wrongful act will not be held liable.

In determining whether an act is the proximate or legal cause of an injury, courts commonly employ one of three tests for causal relation. These tests are referred to as the "but for test," "substantial factor test" and the "probable or foreseeable risk rule." Jurisdictions vary in their application and acceptance of these tests. In determining cause in fact, the first two tests are utilized. When only one causal entity is in question, the "but for" test is employed and where more than one causal entity is in question, the "substantial factor" test is used. The "but for" test holds that a defendant's conduct is not the cause of the injury if the injury would have occurred without it. The "but for" test is sufficient to determine causation in the majority of tort cases. It cannot be used, however, where two or more concurring causes operate to bring about an injury and where any one of the causes operating alone would have brought about the identical result. In cases such as these, the "substantial factor" test is used. This test holds that the defendant's conduct is a cause of the injury if it was a material element and a substantial factor in bringing it about. In both cases, determination of cause is a question for the jury.

In the application of both tests, the jury applies the "more probable than not" standard of proof.

Courts must sometimes entertain a question regarding causal relation where some time lapse exists between an alleged negligent act and an ultimate injury. In situations such as this, the court must determine at which point the law will no longer hold a defendant liable for an injury which he/she has in fact caused. In making this determination, the court applies the "probable or foreseeable consequence rule." There is no question of cause in fact. In applying the test, the court asks whether the injury suffered by the plaintiff was the foreseeable consequence of the original risk created by the negligent act or omission of the defendant. An example of the application of this rule is offered by van der Smissen who reported that a city pool was held liable for an injury resulting from broken glass in a dressing room. The pool allowed a bottle vending machine in the dressing room. The court held that the breaking of bottles was a natural and probable consequence and that injury to barefoot patrons was a foreseeable consequence of the original act of putting the machine in the dressing room.[7]

DAMAGE ISSUE

As previously mentioned, tort law is directed toward the compensation of individuals for losses which they have suffered with respect to any of their legally recognized interests in person or property. The final component of the four part test for negligence requires the plaintiff to show that he/she has actually suffered some harm, loss or injury in order to recover financial compensation from the defendant. It is not enough to show a mere threat of injury nor is it sufficient to show that the defendant has engaged in unreasonable or reckless conduct. Actual injury or loss to one's person or property must be shown or the action fails.

If the plaintiff is able to show that the defendant did in fact owe a duty and that this duty was breached, thereby legally causing injury or harm to him/her, then the plaintiff should be compensated for any losses suffered. Damages, in the legal sense, refer to the monetary compensation meant to cover the losses suffered by the plaintiff in negligence actions. Awarded damages may be of several kinds including compensatory, general, special and punitive.

Compensatory damages are sometimes referred to as actual damages and are designed to compensate the injured party for their actual loss. They typically cover out-of-pocket expenses such as medical bills and loss of wages. General damages are a form of compensatory damages meant to reimburse the injured party for damages which naturally follow the type of conduct carried on by the wrongdoer. Compensation for pain and suffering are typical of general damages.

Special damages are those peculiar to the individual plaintiff including medical expenses and loss of earnings, actual as well as potential. Punitive damages are intended to punish and deter others from the same type of conduct. Punitive damages are noncompensatory and as such fall outside the original philosophical intent of negligence law. Punitive damages normally are not awarded in cases of ordinary negligence but are reserved for cases of intentional torts or gross negligence where the defendant has been shown to have acted with malice, ill will or conscious and reckless disregard for the person and property of others.

There are numerous formulas, rules and guidelines for determining the amount of damages awarded to a given plaintiff. While a judge may guide and control the jury's award, the jury, in the absence of outrageously large or small awards, has fairly wide latitude in their judgments.

DOCTRINE OF RESPONDEAT SUPERIOR
Who Is Liable?

It is not uncommon for a plaintiff to name everyone who is even remotely connected to their injury as defendants in a suit. The basis for this action is the concept of respondeat superior or let the master answer. "The doctrine states that the negligence of the employee is imputed to the corporate entity if the employee was acting within the scope of responsibility and authority, and if not a willful and wanton act to injure another."[8] The doctrine holds an agency accountable for the actions of its employees while also holding the individual employee personally accountable. The doctrine of respondeat superior applies unless limited by statute or common law which either negates or limits the duty owed to the plaintiff. Governmental immunity and limited liability statutes can, in some circumstances, act to eliminate the accountability of the agency for the actions of its employees. Readers are encouraged to check the statutes of their own individual states for further clarification.

While the school district as a corporate entity is held accountable for the actions of its employees, it is not uncommon to see plaintiffs attempt to hold department heads, athletic directors, principals, superintendents and school boards individually liable for the negligent actions of teachers and coaches. In order to hold an administrator or supervisor accountable for the negligent acts of subordinates, the plaintiff must show that the administrator or supervisor either directed or cooperated in some way with the commission of the negligent act. In reality, this amounts to holding administrators liable for their own negligence rather than for that of their subordinates.

As reported by van der Smissen, "acts for which an administrator or supervisor are responsible, and for which negligent performance makes one liable because it enhances the likelihood of injury encompass a wide range of functions. There are five categories of functions:

1. Employing competent personnel and discharging employees shown to be unfit;
2. Providing proper supervision and having a plan of supervision;
3. Directing certain services as to the manner in which they are done;
4. Establishing rules and regulations for safety and complying with policy and statutory requirements; and
5. Remedying dangerous conditions and defective equipment or giving notice of same when there is knowledge of the condition."[9]

Department heads, athletic directors and principals clearly have some responsibility in both the employment and supervision of teaching and coaching staff. In the event of student injury and charges of negligence against teaching and/or coaching staff, the supervisor or administrator overseeing that staff member may likely be charged with individual accountability as well. Where a staff member is charged with negligence, questions about the hiring criteria, the development and communication of building and district policies and procedures, the plan of supervision for building programs and staff, and the supervision of building and equipment maintenance are likely to be asked of all individuals in the organizational chain of command. Neglect in any of these responsibilities, if shown to be a substantial factor in contributing to student injury, can result in a finding of negligence against the supervisor or administrator.

Teachers can find themselves in the role of a supervisor as well when using practicum students, student teachers, teacher aides, and volunteers. It is imperative that teachers in these situations recognize that respondeat superior applies and that they can be held accouintable for the actions of those who are subordinate to them. The teacher retains the ultimate responsibility for his/her classroom. The supervisory responsibility of teachers in these situations needs to be taken seriously and planned for. (This is discussed later in the section on practicum students and student teachers.)

The doctrine of respondeat superior only applies to those actions that occur within the scope of employment. It is important to note that when an individual's actions fall outside the scope of their employment they are left to stand alone and must bear the full responsibility for any liability. (A discussion of scope of employment is included in the section on tangent programs and scope of employment.)

Negligence Defenses

A number of possible defenses may be utilized by a defendant in a court action for negligence. The best and only true affirmative defense against negligence claims is to prove that one or more of the four essential elements of negligence are lacking — that a duty was not owed to the plaintiff, that there was no breach of duty where one existed, that the act in question was not the proximate or legal cause of the injury, or that there was not, in fact, any actual injury or harm.

Aside from the above affirmative defense, a defendant may employ a number of other defenses which, in differing circumstances and jurisdictions, may be effectively used to counter claims of negligence and thereby avoid, or limit, liability. These possible defenses include governmental immunity, procedural noncompliance with tort statutes, assumption of risk, contributory negligence, comparative negligence, last clear chance, and ultra vires act.

The availability of the above defenses varies from jurisdiction to jurisdiction. Readers must investigate the status of governmental immunity and all statutes related to tort legislation in their own states in order to determine the defenses currently available to them. Readers should consult either their school district attorney or their personal attorney for the particulars of the law as it applies in their state.

GOVERNMENTAL IMMUNITY

Sovereign and governmental immunity, whether conferred by constitution, statute or common law, bars actions against the government, its political subdivisions, and in some instances, its officers.

Sovereign immunity refers to the immunity of the state itself, while governmental immunity applies to the legislatively created subdivisions of the state such as municipalities and school districts. Immunity, while not a defense against negligence in the true sense of the word, does provide protection against liability.

Sovereign immunity is an old English common law concept that evolved from the notion that the king could do no wrong. The modern day concept, as applied in American common law, is said by some to have had its origin in 18th century England in the case of Russell v. The Men of Devon, 100 Eng. Rep. 359 (1788). In this case, the entire male population of the unincorporated county of Devon was sued in order to recover damages sustained by a wagon due to the ill-repair of a bridge which the county allegedly had a duty to maintain. The court denied recovery on two counts. First, it claimed there was no law, legislative intent or precedent for an action of this nature; and second, there was no fund out of which the plaintiff could be compensated. The doctrine of immunity arising out of the Russell case was generally accepted by early American courts and was extended so as to cover not only the state but its political subdivisions such as municipalities and school districts as well. Out of the principles laid down in Russell v. The Men of Devon, governmental immunity continued to evolve in the United States.

The rationale for the continued existence of sovereign and governmental immunity includes expediency, protection of public funds, maintenance of the state's supremacy, and the orderly administration of government. Criticism of the doctrine continues in some jurisdictions. Opponents of the doctrine argue that it is inherently unfair, creates governmental irresponsibility, and constitutes an unnecessary exception to the general policy of states whose constitutions guarantee individuals the right to due process.[10] Despite the general criticisms of the doctrine, the U.S. Supreme Court has upheld its constitutionality.

The legislative and judicial trend among the states has been away from immunity as witnessed by the number of states which have abrogated the doctrine either totally or in part. A review of state statutes and case law indicates the overwhelming majority of states have either judicially or statutorily abolished or limited both sovereign and governmental immunity through enactment of tort claims acts and by the authorization to procure liability insurance.

Where not abrogated, sovereign and governmental immunity has typically been limited by tort claims acts in one of five ways. First, legislation has generally placed a statutory limit on the financial liability for any given occurrence of tort. Anywhere from $100,000 to $500,000 has been legislated as a cap by those states that have statutorily limited their liability. In some states, immunity has been waived up to the limits of insurance coverage. Second, some states have limited their liability by distinguishing between their governmental and proprietary functions. In these states governmental functions are held immune to suit while proprietary functions are not. Governmental functions are those which are directly related to the organization's purpose for existing and are often imposed or mandated to the organization by law. Proprietary functions are not directly related to the purpose of the organization. In the K-12 school setting, both physical education and interscholastic athletic programs are held to be governmental functions.

The immunity of governmental agencies has also been limited through the distinction between the discretionary and ministerial duties and acts of their employees and officers. Discretionary duties or acts are those carried out within the scope of employment and in which the individual is required to use personal deliberation, decision and judgment. Ministerial duties or acts are those which the individual is required to perform and in which he/she has no personal discretion. Discretionary refers to functions which are primarily planning in nature while ministerial functions are primarily operational in scope. Discretionary acts are generally protected with immunity in these jurisdictions while ministerial acts are not. The recreational user statutes in a few states have extended immunity for accidents which occur on public school playgrounds during non-school hours. Finally, most jurisdictions still embracing immunity have provided for statutory exceptions which exclude willful and wanton conduct, the maintenance of dangerous facilities and grounds, and the provision of dangerous or defective equipment from immunity protection.

It is important to note that in those jurisdictions which continue to embrace the common law doctrine of governmental immunity, that immunity does not extend to employees who can be sued individually for their own torts. A number of these jurisdictions have statutorily limited the liability of employees, however. Some states have statutorily granted them limited official immunity, holding employees immune for their discretionary acts but not for their ministerial acts. Some statutes hold employees liable for gross negligence and willful and wanton conduct while holding them immune for ordinary negligence.

Other states have enacted hold-harmless statutes which require districts to defend and pay any judgments rendered against employees. Where hold-harmless or indemnification statutes have been enacted, gross negligence or willful and wanton conduct will serve to negate or invalidate their protection. In the case of both statutory official immunity and hold-harmless legislation, only those acts performed within the scope of employment are covered. Any act outside the scope of employment will leave the individual personally liable.

PROCEDURAL NONCOMPLIANCE WITH TORT CLAIMS STATUTES

As previously mentioned, state level tort claims acts have been enacted in a majority of the states to either abrogate or limit the doctrine of governmental immunity. These statutes define the scope of liability for school districts and their employees as well as statutorily set financial caps or limits on liability. They also prescribe some procedural requirements for plaintiffs bringing suits. Failure to comply with the procedural requirements of these statutes can serve as a bar to recovery.

State tort claims acts generally outline the requirements for the filing of a notice of claim and prescribe the statute of limitations for initiating a claim. Nearly two-thirds of the states require that a notice of a claim, generally a written notice, be served within a specified number of days from the time of injury. The number of days specified varies from jurisdiction to jurisdiction ranging anywhere from 90 days to three years. The primary reason for the notice requirement is to allow a timely investigation of the claims while the facts are fresh and witnesses are available, and to allow for a negotiated settlement without litigation. While not all states require a notice of claim to be submitted, all states do have statutes of limitation which restrict the length of time in which a suit may actually be filed. Tort claims usually have a two or three year statute of limitation, with two years being the most common.

Most tort claim acts have built in an exception to both the notice of claim and statute of limitation requirements for minors or for those who are incapacitated either physically or mentally. The built-in exceptions serve to lengthen the time frame involved.

CONTRIBUTORY NEGLIGENCE

Section 463 of the Restatement of Torts defines contributory negligence as "conduct on the part of the plaintiff which falls below the standard to which he/she should conform for his/her own protection, and which is a legally contributing cause cooperating with the negligence of the defendant in bringing about the plaintiff's harm."[11] Contributory negligence is a harsh concept in that any showing of negligence on the part of the plaintiff, even slight, will bar the plaintiff from any recovery of damages. "The defense does not rest upon the idea that the defendant is relieved of any duty toward the plaintiff. Rather, although the defendant has violated his/her duty, has been negligent, and would otherwise be liable, the plaintiff is denied recovery because his/her own conduct disentitles him/her to maintain the action."[12]

In a few circumstances, the plaintiff who is guilty of contributory negligence is not barred from recovering damages. These circumstances include cases where the defendant is guilty of willful, wanton and reckless conduct and in cases of intentional torts.

The burden of proof for contributory negligence rests with the defendant and, in most states, must be proven by a preponderance of the evidence. In determining the reasonableness of a plaintiff's actions, the same standard of care used for defendants is applied. The plaintiff is required to act as a reasonably prudent person of like age, capacity and experience would act in the same or similar circumstances and to take reasonable precautions to guard their own safety. Basically, the same four elements necessary for negligence apply to contributory negligence. The same special allowances are made for plaintiffs, as for defendants, who are limited by physical or mental disability or age.

Contributory negligence on the part of children is much more difficult to establish than in the case of adults. Drawing from a review of case law, van der Smissen summarizes that "some states use a guideline of below seven years of age not capable of contributory negligence, over 14 years of age capable of contributory negligence, and between ages (8-13) dependent upon the circumstances and the individual."[13]

As a harsh concept, contributory negligence has come to be viewed somewhat unfavorably by the courts but, nonetheless, still lingers on in a handful of jurisdictions. The majority of jurisdictions have slowly moved away from this concept and have offset the drastic consequences of contributory negligence by developing and implementing the concept of last clear chance and comparative negligence.

LAST CLEAR CHANCE

Last clear chance is an occassionaly accepted modification of the strict and harsh rule of contributory negligence. It allows a plaintiff who is guilty of contributory negligence to recover damages if it is shown that the defendant had the last clear opportunity to avoid the harm or injury.

The reasoning behind the last clear chance doctrine is a source of much discussion and debate. It has been argued that if a defendant had the last clear chance to avoid the harm, then the plaintiff's negligence could not be the proximate or legal cause of the resulting injury. Other courts have reasoned that whoever had the last clear chance to avoid the injury possessed the higher degree of fault and should carry the burden of liability — a hint of comparative negligence principles.

A plaintiff can be found in one of two basic predicaments, helpless peril and inattentive peril. Helpless peril refers to situations where the plaintiff's contributory negligence has placed them in a predicament from which they cannot remove themselves. Inattentive peril pertains to those situations where the plaintiff's contributory negligence has placed them in a predicament from which they could remove themselves through the use of ordinary or reasonable care, but where they negligently remain right up to the time of injury.

Under the doctrine of last clear chance, the defendant has slightly different obligations and liability within the above two situations. In both cases, where the defendant discovers the plaintiff in either helpless or inattentive peril and has the opportunity to avoid the accident but fails to do so, the plaintiff is not barred from recovering damages. Where the defendant fails to discover the plaintiff in peril, however, the law makes a distinction between the two predicaments. In the case of the plaintiff in helpless peril, the court will ask whether the defendant could or would have discovered the helpless peril through the use of reasonable care. In this situation, the court treats "should have discovered" as "did discover." Where the defendant fails to discover inattentive peril, very few courts have permitted the plaintiff to recover any damages. The courts reason that the negligence of both plaintiff and defendant made them ignorant of each other in this situation, and therefore, neither of them had the last clear chance to avoid harm. The plaintiff is thereby barred from recovering damages under the doctrine of contributory negligence.[14]

ASSUMPTION OF RISK

The assumption of risk concept assumes that a plaintiff recognizes the danger in a given situation and voluntarily assumes the risk, thereby relieving the defendant of any duty to protect the plaintiff. It requires both the actual knowledge and understanding of the risk and the voluntary assumption of it. If either of these factors is missing, the defense fails. Knowledge and understanding of the risks are generally limited to the normal hazards associated with a given activity, as a plaintiff would not be expected to adequately comprehend risks beyond those. A spectator at a baseball game, for example, can be said to assume the risk of being hit by a foul ball but certainly does not assume the risk of bleachers collapsing.

Individuals may assume risks either expressly or through implication. Express assumption occurs when parties enter into agreements limiting their liability to one another. These agreements can take a couple of forms. Individuals can enter into written agreements whereby they agree to assume the known and inherent risks involved in a given activity. They can also execute waiver or release agreements whereby they assume not only the inherent risks of the activity but also the risk of ordinary negligence by the other party to the agreement. The law requires that the risks being waived are both clear and understood.

There are situations where the law will not allow such express assumption of risk. Courts generally hold waiver and release agreements in the K-12 school setting to be invalid. Waiver and release agreements represent contracts. As minors cannot legally enter into contracts, they are not in any position to sign away their rights. While these agreements are often signed by parents or guardians, the law has long recognized that a parent may not sign away the legal rights of their minor children. In the case of students who reach legal age while in school, the courts still limit the validity of such agreements. A six-part test used by courts in determining the validity of waiver and release agreements is outlined in Wagenblast v. Odessa School District, 758 P.2d 968 (1988) in the section on miscellaneous issues (page 173). The implications of waivers and releases related to implied assumption and contributory negligence are also discussed at that point.

Implied assumption occurs in those situations where the plaintiff becomes aware of and understands and appreciates the given risks, yet voluntarily proceeds to confront those risks. In doing so, he/she is said to have decided to take their chances and liability of any defendant is waived. The conduct of the plaintiff is viewed as an agreement to assume the risk. Implied assumption of risk is not an appropriate defense in the physical education setting where participation is generally not voluntary. It is, however, commonly employed in cases involving interscholastic athletics. Again, any assumed risk must be inherent to the activity, known and compre-hended by the participant, and voluntarily assumed. As noted by Baker, the "voluntary assumption of risk, either express or implied, must be adjusted to consideration of age and capacity of the indivi-dual to cope with the risks involved."[15]

Most tort actions entertained by the courts involve cases of implied assumption. The issue of assumption of risk is one for the jury, and juries have proven to be somewhat sensitive to the plight of the injured plaintiff and do not assign assumption of risk lightly. It is never upheld as a defense in cases involving young children or those incapable of comprehending the risks involved in a given activity.

Assumption of risk, like contributory negligence, is a harsh doctrine. In those jurisdictions which still adhere to the concept, any finding of assumption of risk will act as a total bar to recovery. A good number of states have judicially or statutorily abolished the doctrine while integrating some of the concepts into the more equitable doctrine of comparative negligence.

COMPARATIVE NEGLIGENCE

The intent of comparative negligence or comparative fault, as it is often referred, is to apportion the damages between the negligent plaintiff and the negligent defendant. Because of a general dissatisfaction with the doctrine of contributory negligence and the harshness it exerts on injured plaintiffs who to some degree contributed to their own injury, the majority of states have enacted comparative fault statutes which have served to abolish contributory negligence and implied assumption of risk as total bars to recovery. The principles discussed under both contributory negligence and assumption of risk are still employed by the courts in determining the degree of fault to be assigned to an injured plaintiff who contributed in some manner to his/her own injury. Comparative fault statutes are generally viewed as an attempt to more fairly dispense justice in tort actions.

Comparative negligence or fault statutes vary in their approach from state to state. Some jurisdictions have adopted a pure approach to comparative fault which strictly assigns percentage of fault to both the plaintiff and the defendant with no restrictions. Under this approach, if a defendant was found to be 10% at fault while the plaintiff 90% at fault, the plaintiff would collect 10% of the assigned damages. Other states have adopted a more restrictive or modified approach to comparative fault. Some of these states allow contributorily negligent plaintiffs to recover damages only if their negligence was slight in comparison with the gross negligence of the defendant. Most states have adopted an approach which allows recovery provided the plaintiff is not more than 50% negligent in causing his/her own injuries. For example, if the plaintiff was 40% at fault and the defendant 60% at fault, the plaintiff would receive 40% of any award. However, if the plaintiff was found to be 55% at fault and the defendant 45% at fault, the plaintiff would receive nothing.

ULTRA VIRES ACT

The defense of ultra vires act is used to negate the doctrine of respondeat superior. Whereas the doctrine of respondeat superior serves to hold a school district liable for the negligent acts of its employees, school districts will argue that they should not be held responsible for those actions of employees which fall outside the scope of their responsibility or authority (ultra vires act).

Most states that have enacted tort claims legislation have specifically limited their liability to those damages arising out of actions which fall within the scope of employment. Hold-harmless or indemnification statutes likewise exclude ultra vires acts from protection and district insurance coverage is always written to cover only those actions falling within the scope of employment. Whenever injury occurs as a result of employee actions deemed to be outside the scope of employment, the employee will be left to stand alone in suit and must rely on his/her own resources and insurance for protection.

Duties of Physical Education and Sport Staff

The duties owed to students by physical education and sport staff are set by both common law and statute. Common law duty represents the degree of care the community requires to be exercised for the protection of others. The standard of care required to avoid liability is that of a reasonably prudent person in the same or similar circumstances.

Statutory law, together with common law, requires that physical education and sport staff provide adequate and proper instruction, supervision, inspection of equipment, grounds and facilitites, transportation, and the rendering of first aid when necessary. Specific duties and responsibilities under each of these areas are numerous and an abundance of case law has helped delineate them.

Vast numbers of court actions involving school districts and their employees are threatened each year. Due to the large number of participants and the unique opportunities for physical and social interaction, physical education and sport are particularly vulnerable to court action. From the large numbers of threatened actions, a small percentage of claims go to trial, as a good number are settled out of court. From the cases which go to trial, an even smaller percentage end up in appellate or supreme courts for review. While records of original trial courts are kept, the only access to these records is by case name at the courthouse. No indexing or reporting system for trial court actions exists. Therefore, the legal researcher, when examining case law, is limited for the most part to appellate or supreme court decisions as reported in the National, Regional and

State Reporter systems. Trial court decisions which are appealed are done so on the basis of a point of law rather than on issues of fact. Most of the reported discussion, therefore, centers on these points of law rather than on the facts and circumstances of the alleged negligent behavior or act.

While it is recognized that individual state approaches to negligence and tort claims legislation differ from jurisdiction to jurisdiction, a review of case law from across the country will give physical education and sport staff a practical and useful glimpse at the type of teacher/coach actions and facility conditions which have been challenged in court. Matching the fact situations and holdings in these cases to the legal concepts already discussed and the law as it exists in the state of the reader, should provide physical education and sport staff with some practical insight on what might occur in their state.

INSTRUCTION AND TEACHING METHODOLOGY

Claims of negligent instruction can cover a broad range of complaints including improper instruction, insufficient instructions and improper teaching methodology. Aside from claims of improper supervision, physical education and sport staff are most commonly pulled into court over claims of negligent instruction.

The rapid expansion of programs over the past two decades and the increased demand for accountability in programs has led to the requirement for expertise by physical education and sport staff in a growing variety of activities. Physical education and sport staff must thoroughly understand all activities which they undertake to teach or coach and must continue to refine their skill and knowledge through inservice opportunities, conferences, clinics and workshops. It is especially critical that they upgrade their skill and knowledge in areas of weakness before undertaking the delivery of those areas of the curriculum or activity program to students.

When instructing a student or athlete to carry out a task, physical educators and coaches must be sure that their instructions are proper under the given set of circumstances. Instructions must conform to recognized standards employed within the professional field and with recommended practices for specific activities. When giving instruction in any area of the physical education curriculum or sport program, teachers and coaches will be held to the standard of a reasonably prudent person qualified to teach or coach that area. The courts will look at more than certification when determining one's qualifications. Physical education and sport staff can expect to be challenged whenever their instructions deviate from the recognized standards for the questioned activity or from district, state or activity association guidelines.

It is not only important that a teacher's/coach's instructions be proper but that they also be sufficient in detail to allow students or athletes to carry out the instructions and participate in a safe manner. In viewing the sufficiency of instruction, courts examine the skill instructions, including instructor and/or student demonstrations, as well as safety instructions. While striving to cut down on talk and maximize physical movement and participation in physical education and sport, physical educators and coaches are cautioned not to short-change the adequacy or completeness of their instructions.

Coercing students to perform can be a very dangerous practice for both physical educators and coaches. Claims of coercion, together with improper instruction, have been dealt with by the courts. Physical education and sport staff would be prudent not to second-guess student fears about performing a skill or to coerce them to execute skills after minimal instruction. Under some circumstances, coercion has been viewed by the courts as constituting willful and wanton misconduct.

A good number of the skills taught in physical education and sport are sequential in nature. Considerable attention needs to be given to the logical and safe sequencing of skills to allow for not only safe but successful participation. This is especially important in those developmental activities with elevated risk, such as gymnastics. Planning for proper sequencing should not be left to chance. Physical educators and coaches would be prudent to prepare not only written daily lesson or practice plans, but unit plans as well. These documents should be kept on file as courts have sometimes requested that instructors produce them in order for the court to examine the methodology and sequencing employed in the class or activity. While daily written lesson plans are extremely important, the often neglected unit plan offers the best opportunity to satisfactorily plan for both the successful and safe learning by students and athletes.

Physical education and sport staff need to thoroughly acquaint themselves with district and state scope and sequence documents, curriculum materials, activity and sport guidelines, and safety materials. When the adequacy and propriety of a teacher's/coach's instruction are challenged, these documents and the teacher's or coach's awareness of and compliance with them often become factors examined by the courts.

The cases which follow offer practical illustrations of the several instructional issues discussed above which have been examined by the courts.

Larson v. Independent School District No. 314
289 N.W. 2d 112

> Issue: Improper instruction and methodology —
> Lack of unit plan and progressions in gymnastics

Level of Court: State Supreme Court
Date/State: 1979/Minnesota
Decision: Plaintiff/Affirmed

An eighth grade student was injured while performing a headspring over a rolled mat in a required physical education class. As a result of landing on his head and from the force of running and diving onto the mat, the plaintiff broke his neck, resulting in quadraplegic paralysis. Plaintiff brought action against the teacher, principal and superintendent claiming negligence in instruction and supervision.

Testimony showed that the teacher involved was a first-year teacher who had only been on the job nine class periods before the accident occurred. He had replaced the previous teacher at mid-year when the previous teacher had to report for military duty. The plaintiff alleged negligence in instruction and supervision based on the argument that the teacher taught a difficult gymnastic skill without first teaching appropriate lead-up skills or progressions, designed in part for safety, and that the teacher was improperly spotting at the time of the accident. Negligence claims against the principal and superintendent were based on their alleged failure to properly develop, administer and supervise the physical education program. Testimony showed that the principal did not actively participate in developing or supervising the physical education curriculum and that these duties were totally delegated to the first-year teacher. The principal's only involvement was to hand the new teacher a copy of the curriculum guide. He merely asked that the two teachers meet and plan physical education classes for the remainder of the year. The two teachers met for 30 minutes and discussed which units had been taught and which had not. When reporting for duty, the teacher told the principal what subjects he was going to teach. No detailed discussion of activities or teaching methods occurred.

Expert testimony indicated that unit planning in physical education was of critical importance in ensuring that proper progressions for safety were followed and that such planning should be in addition to daily lesson plans. Neither the new nor previous teacher were required to develop or submit any such detailed written plans.

The court found for the plaintiff, declaring the teacher 90 percent negligent, the principal 10 percent negligent and the student free from negligence. A directed verdict was issued on behalf of the superintendent on the grounds that a prima facie case of negligence on his part had not been established. The plaintiff was awarded $1,013,630 and his father $142,937.

In upholding the trial court decision for the plaintiff, the Supreme Court ruled:

1. The evidence supported a finding of negligence in the instruction and supervision of the physical education class by the first-year teacher.
2. The record indicated that the principal failed to exercise reasonable care in supervising the development, planning and supervision of the physical education program and in supervising a first-year teacher.
3. Neither the principal, in his abdication of responsibility for developing and administering the program, nor the teacher, in deciding how to teach and spot an advanced gymnastic skill, were involved in decision making entitled to protection under the doctrine of discretionary immunity.

4. Where found personally liable, the defendants
   were not entitled to indemnity under governmental immunity
5. In purchasing insurance, the district waived its
   absolute claim to governmental immunity up to
   the limits of its coverage.

Due to the purchase of liability insurance, the court held the
school vicariously liable for the torts of its employees and ordered it
to pay $50,000 to each plaintiff.

Ehlinger v. Board of Education of
New Hartford Central School
465 N.Y.S. 2d 378

> Issue: Improper instruction — Failure to follow
> recommendations for fitness test administration

Level of Court: State Supreme Court, Appellate Division
Date/State: 1983/New York
Decision: Defendant/Remand for new trial

Plaintiff brought action on behalf of her 14-year-old daughter
who dislocated her right elbow when she struck the wall while
running the speed test portion of the New York State physical fitness
test in her physical education class. The plaintiff alleged that the
defendant was negligent in failing to follow the recommendations in
the test manual for designing the course and failing to provide adequate instructions and supervision for those taking the test. Testimony
showed that the manual recommended a minimum of 14 feet clearance beyond both the start and finish lines and that the defendant, in
setting up the course, only provided eight feet of clearance. The only
instructions given were for the students to run around the cones
three times and for their partner to record their times. The clearance
beyond the start and finish lines was reduced due to the class being
held in the "girls" gym which was smaller than standard size.

The court ruled there was a duty owed to the plaintiff by the
defendant to act as a reasonably prudent person under comparable
circumstances. The court held that a jury could certainly find it
foreseeable that injury would result from running the course as

designed, and in light of the defendant's failure to follow the recommendations in the manual or warn students of possible safety hazards due to course modification, the jury could conclude that this duty was breached. The court reversed the dismissal judgment of the lower court and ordered a new trial.

Green v. Orleans Parish School Board
365 So. 2d 834

Issue: Adequacy of instruction — Lead-up to wrestling match

Level of Court: State Court of Appeals
Date/State: 1978/Court of Appeals
Decision: Defendant/Affirmed

The plaintiff, who had gone out for football, failed to pass the vision test required by the board and was not allowed to engage in contact activities. He did participate in exercises and noncontact drills. The plaintiff was transferred into sixth period physical education in accordance with the coach's policy of having the football players take physical education together.

After two weeks of spring training, the sixth period physical education class began a six-week unit in wrestling and weight lifting. The first three classes in wrestling consisted of warm ups and instruction in basic positions and moves. Each move was demonstrated and then practiced "by the numbers," in which each move was broken down and executed methodically step-by-step. On the fourth day, students were directed to wrestle hard for 30 seconds using the basic moves they were taught. Each 30-second match was officiated by a varsity wrestler.

While attempting to roll out of a bridge, the plaintiff injured his neck and was left paralyzed. The plaintiff filed suit against the district claiming inadequate instruction and supervision. The Court of Appeals upheld the trial court finding of no negligence on the part of the defendants. The trial court noted that the duty of instructing, preparing, and supervising students in dangerous activities was to use due care to minimize the risk of harm. The court ruled that the conditioning was adequate and the students had been properly prepared through instruction in the basic moves to take part in the drill. The class was held to be properly organized and supervised.

The Court of Appeals noted that the plaintiff's lengthy expert testimony was impressive; however, the defendant's presentation of expert testimony was just as impressive. The appellate court stated that the trial court had not "erred manifestly in finding the evidence did not preponderate in favor of the conclusion that the teacher's instruction, preparation for, and supervision of the drill in which the plaintiff was injured fell below any locally or nationally accepted standard of reasonable care for teachers under similar circumstances."

Note: This case is an example of a teacher doing a lot of things right. The class had undergone two weeks of conditioning before the wrestling unit began, had undergone a warm-up, and had received instructions, including demonstration, of the skills to be learned. The skills were broken down into small components and practiced for three days before being applied in a short match. This sequencing demonstrated an awareness of and appreciation for student safety. In any activity, particularly a contact activity or one of elevated risk, instruction should include safety instructions and a warning about risks inherent in the activity, especially those risks associated with the improper performance of required tasks.

Stehn v. Bernarr MacFadden Foundations, Inc.
434 F. 2d 811

Issue: Improper instruction and supervision of wrestling

Level of Court: U.S. Court of Appeals
Date/State: 1970/Tennessee
Decision: Plaintiff/Affirmed

The plaintiff suffered a broken neck resulting in quadraplegia as a result of participating in a wrestling match in class. Trial court evidence established that the eighth-grade boy had been in the wrestling class for six weeks and attended class four times a week. At the time of the accident the 137-pound plaintiff was wrestling a 150-pound boy. Two matches were going on at the time with the plaintiff's match being refereed by another student. The plaintiff was in the down referee's position when the round started. The boy in the up position attempted to immediately turn the plaintiff from his front to his back using the "agura" move. This move was taught by the instructor although the term "agura" was unknown to the expert witnesses and was not found in texts on the sport. The plaintiff testified that while taught how to perform the move, students were not taught how to counteract it defensively. The plaintiff had wrestled a previous match to the one in which he was injured and had approximately seven minutes of rest between matches. The first match was also against a heavier opponent.

The defendant moved for a directed verdict at the conclusion of the trial. The trial court denied the motion and the jury returned a verdict for the plaintiff and awarded $385,000 in damages. The defendant appealed charging that the evidence was insufficient to support a verdict against it. The Court of Appeals upheld the lower court decision while ruling that adequate standards were provided against which the jury could compare the quality of instruction and supervision and the manner in which the class was conducted. The court ruled that the evidence created a proper question for jury determination which precluded a directed verdict. While holding that no single factor in the plaintiff's charges would establish a breach of duty in and of itself, the court ruled that the defendant's conduct in each of the following areas was relevant and could be used by the jury in deciding whether the instruction and supervision were proper. Specifically, the jury was free to examine and weight the following factors in making its determination:

1. The number of pupils in the class;
2. The number of matches being supervised by the instructor at one time;
3. The training and experience of the teacher/coach;
4. The use of other students as referees;
5. The weight difference between wrestlers; and
6. Number of matches allowed per student and the amount of rest between matches.

Note. The court in this case listed a number of factors that could be considered by the jury in making its determination on negligence. It is important to note that while any individual factor may not prove fatal to a defendant in a negligence action, the interaction of two or more factors can often result in a finding of negligent behavior. In this case, it is quite possible that the interaction of multiple factors contributed to the jury's finding. For example, while the weight difference between the two wrestlers and the rest period between matches were two separate issues, the interplay between the two could conceivably be what contributed to the injury.

Armlin v. Board of Education of Middleburgh Central School District
320 N.Y.S. 2d 402

> Issue: Supervision and instruction in
> multiple station gymnastics class

Level of Court: Supreme Court, Appellate Division
Date/State: 1971/New York
Decision: Plaintiff/Affirmed

A fifth grade student was injured in her physical education class as a result of a fall from the rings. Evidence indicated that the rings were high enough to be out of reach of the plaintiff and that a mat was placed underneath. At the time of the accident, there were six different pieces of apparatus on the floor with the 35 girls in class divided equally amongst the six stations. The accident occurred when the girl stood up in the rings and, while jumping out, fell backwards and landed on her back.

The plaintiff testified at trial that she had dismounted from the rings in the same manner on numerous other occasions and had seen other students do the same. At no time did the teacher object to what the girls were doing. The plaintiff testified the girls were told they could do anything they wanted on the rings except swing. Testimony indicated that the teacher never demonstrated any stunts on any of the apparatus and that while spotters were provided, they never received any instruction on spotting procedures.

The teacher testified that she did not see what the plaintiff was doing or see her fall. She also testified that standing up in the rings and jumping out backwards would be dangerous and that in so doing, the girls "could kill themselves." The state physical education syllabus stated that in a fifth grade gymnastics class, "the apparatus and the class should be so placed as to be entirely in view of the teacher."

The Appellate Court upheld the lower court finding of negligence. It ruled that a fair interpretation of the evidence allowed a reasonable jury to conclude that the teacher was negligent in conducting, instructing and supervising the physical education class.

Fosselman v. Waterloo Community School District
229 N.W. 2d 280

Issue: Appropriateness of game — Bombardment

Level of Court: Supreme Court
Date/State: 1975/Iowa
Decision: Defendant/Affirmed

The plaintiff received multiple facial fractures as a result of his participation in the game of bombardment in his physical education class. Bombardment is a game of dodgeball which begins by placing a number of balls on the centerline of a court, lining up opposing teams on opposite ends of the court, and on a command to start, having players race to the center to grab a ball. Players who get control of a ball must return to a designated line before they may start to throw the ball at opposing team members. When hit by a ball, a player is out of the game. The plaintiff received his injuries when he charged the centerline to grab a ball and he struck his face on the knee of an opposing player charging from the other direction. The teacher was either participating or observing from the side of the court but in either case, he did not see the accident happen.

Suit was brought against the school district, the board of directors, the individual members of the board, the superintendent, the director of health and physical education, the principal and the teacher. The claim charged that the defendants were negligent in permitting the game to be played and in requiring the plaintiff to participate and also charged they were negligent in their supervision of the class. The defendants filed a motion to have the case dimissed. The trial judge ordered the case dismissed against all defendants except the teacher. The charge of negligence against the teacher for permitting the game to be played when he knew or should have known that it was dangerous and likely to cause injury was allowed to go to trial. The jury returned a verdict in favor of the defendant.

The Supreme Court upheld the lower court dismissal of charges related to supervision holding that no evidence was introduced which would have suggested any increased supervision could have prevented the accident. The court held that in his appeal, the plaintiff failed to cite any authority to justify overturning the jury verdict in favor of the teacher. The court noted that significant evidence was introduced by the defendant that indicated the game bombardment was played in the surrounding schools and was recognized as a proper activity in physical education classes. The court ruled that the jury verdict was not contrary to the evidence.

Note. While the game of bombardment is not an inappropriate activity in and of itself, steps can be taken to make the activity safer and more enjoyable for students. Anticipating the risk of collisions, the teacher in this case could have easily modified the procedure for beginning the game without altering the objectives and intent of the activity. It would seem plausible that a number of courts might find that having students charge head-on after a ball placed on the center line might foreseeably result in collisions and injury. The duty of physical education teachers is to foresee risks and to take *reasonable* steps to reduce a risk where it exists.

Passantino v. Board of Education of the City of New York
395 N.Y.S. 2d 628

Issue: Inadequate instruction — Collision between base runner and catcher

---

Level of Court: Court of Appeals
Date/State: 1977/New York
Decision: Plaintiff/Remanded re: damages/Reversed
                and dismissed

The plaintiff suffered injuries resulting in quadraplegia as a result of colliding with the catcher as he was running home. Trial evidence established that the plaintiff was a junior with four years experience in the game of baseball and well versed in the fundamentals of the game. On the day of the accident, while the plaintiff was on third base, the coach called for a squeeze play, requiring the plaintiff to begin stealing home as soon as the pitcher had committed himself and the batter to bunt the ball. The batter, instead of bunting, took a full swing and missed. The plaintiff had traveled one third of the way home and was moving at full speed as the catcher, in possession of the ball, took several steps toward third and waited for the tag out. The plaintiff chose not to return to third and as he came within about five feet of the catcher lowered his head, rammed the catcher at full speed and, thereby, suffered his injuries. Plaintiff alleged that the defendants were negligent in:

1. Carelessly training and supervising him, as well as the activity;
2. Failing to provide adequate and competent coaching; and
3. Failing to properly instruct in the fundamentals of baseball.

The jury found for the plaintiff and awarded $1,800,000 in damages. The Supreme Court, Appellate Division upheld the lower court decision for the plaintiff but found the award of damages to be excessive and ordered a new trial relative to damages unless the plaintiff agreed to reduce the damages to $1,000,000. Judge Cohalan dissented from the majority and voted to reverse the lower court decision. In his opinion, the evidence indicated that the plaintiff had assumed the risk of injury and was contributorily negligent in that he failed to either return to third or slide home and chose to use his head as a battering ram instead.

After reviewing the record, particularly the dissenting opinion, the Court of Appeals reversed the decision of the lower courts and dismissed the complaint. The Court ruled that the defendant's motion at the end of the trial for a dismissal should have been granted as the evidence failed to establish a prima facie case of negligence on the part of the defendants.

Note: Since this case was decided, the duty to warn has been increasingly argued before courts relative to sport injuries. A Seattle case involving the failure to warn about the use of a helmet in "spearing" brought this issue into clear focus and resulted in a $6.3 million judgment against the Seattle School District. The issue of failure to warn has somewhat lessened the force of the assumption of risk defense as was used in this case. To assume a risk, the risk must be known and appreciated by the injured party. As sliding in baseball can involve substantial contact, much like that when warding off a tackler in football, warnings about the use of the head as a battering ram or point of contact should be given. These warnings should sufficiently inform athletes of the specific risk and consequences of any failure to adhere to that warning.

Passafaro v. Board of Education of the City of New York
353 N.Y.S. 2d 178

> Issue: Improper instructions — Going barefoot in gym

Level of Court: Supreme Court, Appellate Division
Date/State: 1974/New York
Decision: Plaintiff/Reversed and granted new trial

The plaintiff was awarded $50,000 for injuries he sustained as a result of slipping on the gym floor while participating in gymnastics during his physical education class. Testimony was conflicting regarding the instructions given to the plaintiff. The plaintiff alleged that the physical education teacher told him to participate in his stocking feet because he forgot his tennis shoes. The defendant denied giving such an instruction and testified that the plaintiff was directed to stay at the side of the gym and observe the class. The evidence established, and the defendant agrees, that participating in stocking feet is a bad practice. A substantial question of fact regarding the given instructions was presented to the jury.

The charge given to the jury instructed that recovery could be predicated on the improper instruction to exercise in stocking feet or in the failure to provide adequate or sufficient supervision for the students in the class. The jury found in favor of the plaintiff and the defendant appealed.

On appeal, the defendant claimed that the suit brought by the plaintiff was based on giving improper instructions and that the court's charge to the jury regarding supervision was, therefore, improper. The Supreme Court agreed with the defendant and ruled that, although the plaintiff injected evidence of inadequate supervision while charging the teacher with giving improper instructions, the evidence submitted at the trial cannot support a conclusion of insufficient supervision and the judgment must be reversed. Even if the evidence of inadequate supervision was sufficient, the court noted that the plaintiff, by his own admission, attributed the accident to his required participation in stockings.

The court held that improper supervision could not have been the proximate cause of the injury regardless of whose testimony the jury accepted, as the student slipped before reaching the mat where the activity was being conducted and where student leaders and spotters were present and was instructed, according to the defendant, to not participate in the first place. Finally, the court ruled that the school board was not an "insurer of student safety and was not required to provide such continuous supervision that it could control the movements of all students, at all times." The lower court judgment against the defendant was reversed and a new trial granted.

Landers v. School District No. 203, O'Fallon
383 N.E. 2d 645

> Issue: Improper instruction — Coercion to perform gymnastic skill

Level of Court: State Appellate Court
Date/State: 1978/Illinois
Decision: Plaintiff/Affirmed

The plaintiff, a 15-year-old high school student, was injured in her physical education class while attempting to do a backward roll. Testimony indicated that at the time of the accident, one week after the tumbling unit began, the plaintiff was 5'6" tall and weighed approximately 180 pounds. She was in a class with approximately 40 other girls.

The instructor had students observe another student prior to practicing the backward roll. Prior to the accident, the plaintiff received no personal instruction or attention from the teacher with respect to the backward roll. The plaintiff testified that the day prior to the accident, she went to the instructor's office and told the teacher she was afraid to do the backward roll and that she did not know how to perform it. She claimed to have told the teacher that as a small child she completed the move a half dozen times, but not properly, and that the activity always gave her a headache and bothered her neck. She informed the instructor she was afraid to perform the skill because she was big and heavy. The teacher offered to help the plaintiff after school but was unable to do so because the plaintiff was a bus student. The following day, after asking the plaintiff if she could do the backward roll and being told no, the teacher told her to practice it and have another student help her. In doing so, the plaintiff suffered a subluxation of her vertebrae. She eventually had to have a cervical fusion, grafting bone from her hip onto four vertebrae in the neck.

Illinois law confers the status of in loco parentis on teachers which results in teachers being subjected to no greater liability for their acts than are parents. Therefore, under Illinois law, teachers are only liable for their acts or omissions which are deemed to constitute willful or wanton misconduct. They are not liable for mere negligence.

The trial court held the teacher's conduct to constitute willful and wanton misconduct. In so holding, the court stated that the teacher was aware that the plaintiff was obese, untrained in the skill being demanded, fearful of performing it due to her size and because she had experienced physical problems in the past from attempting to perform the skill. The court ruled that, given these circumstances, the teacher's demand that she do the skill anyway, without any personal instruction or testing of her strength, showed an utter indifference to the plaintiff's safety. The Appellate Court upheld the trial court judgment of $77,000 for the plaintiff.

Note. Second guessing student fears about performing certain tasks can be very risky business. As a teacher or coach, it would be prudent to back up in the progression of skills taught to be sure that the students are physically prepared for and capable of performing the required task. Along these same lines, teachers and coaches should not second guess any student complaints about illness or injury. While some students clearly manufacture illness and injury excuses to get out of performing certain tasks, in the event of an injury, the teacher or coach would appear foolish in court trying to explain why he/she chose to ignore a student complaint and required the student to perform. Coercion is a poor and risky strategy in both of the situations above.

District School Board of Lake County v. Talmadge
381 So. 2d 698

Issue: Improper instruction — Coercion to perform
on trampoline

Level of Court: State Supreme Court
Date/State: 1980/Florida
Decision: Dismissed/Reversed and remanded/Affirmed

The plaintiff, a middle school student, brought suit against the school board, its insurance company and the physical education teacher for injuries sustained while performing on the trampoline in his physical education class. The plaintiff alleged the physical education teacher ordered him to perform certain skills on the trampoline. When he refused, the teacher physically picked him up, placed him on the trampoline and again ordered him to perform. When the plaintiff attempted a forward flip, he injured his knee and teeth. The evidence indicated that the teacher provided the plaintiff with minimal skill and safety instructions on the trampoline and that the plaintiff had little experience on the equipment and was, therefore, unprepared to safely perform the skills demanded by the teacher.

The trial court dismissed the suit claiming that Florida statutes do not allow a cause of action to exist against the teacher. The Court of Appeals reversed the dismissal against the instructor, holding that Florida statute indemnifies employees of the state against monetary judgments rendered against them as a result of negligent acts occurring within the scope of their employment but does not bar holding an employee as a party defendant. The court remanded the case against the teacher for proceedings consistent with the above ruling. The district and teacher appealed the Appellant Court's decision to the Florida Supreme Court.

The Florida Supreme Court upheld the lower court's decision holding that the absence of an explicit prohibition in Florida statutes against suing public employees for their torts suggests that none was intended. The court ruled that the hold harmless statute did not preclude a public employee from being named a defendant in tort action.

The court made note that, where a public employee's acts fell outside of the scope of their employment or constituted willful and wanton misconduct, the employee is individually liable and the state need not pay judgments rendered against the employee. Where the district and the teacher are sued jointly, the state is obligated to pay up to the monetary limits of liability imposed by state statute and the teacher is personally liable for any excess.

Peterson v. Multnomah County School District No. 1
668 P. 2d 385

> Issue: Inadequate amount of practice prior to
> first contact scrimmage

Level of Court: Court of Appeals
Date/State: 1983/Oregon
Decision: Plaintiff/Affirmed

A high school football player suffered a neck injury during football practice which left him a quadraplegic. Trial evidence indicated the player was a 15-year-old sophomore participating in a contact scrimmage on what was only the second day of preseason practice. The contact scrimmage ran contrary to a school district advisory which advised against any contact during the first week of practice. The injury occurred as a result of using the helmet as the point of contact when tackling another player. While evidence indicated that the team was warned about the use of "spearing" before practice began, it was alleged that the injured player had used the same technique on previous plays and had received praise by the coaching staff for his hard-hitting tackles.

Two years after suit was filed against the school district, the plaintiff filed an amended complaint adding the Oregon School Activities Association (OSAA) as a defendant. The OSAA is a private nonprofit corporation which, as a member of the National Federation of State High School Associations, operates to regulate a variety of matters related to school activities and competition between member schools.

While the National Federation adopted safety recommendations relative to contact scrimmages in preseason football, which were developed by a joint committee of the National Federation and the American Medical Association, the OSAA did not adopt the recommendations as requirements for its member schools and did not forward the recommendations on to member schools. One of the recommendations was that practice games or "game condition scrimmages" be prohibited during the first two weeks of practice.

The school district settled with the plaintiff out of court prior to trial and awarded the plaintiff $100,000, which is the statutory limit on the liability of school districts and its employees under the Oregon Tort Claims Act.

The case continued against OSAA charging that it was negligent for failing to require or to recommend member schools undertake safety measures related to football practice, specifically, that contact scrimmages not take place during the first week of practice and that "spearing" be prohibited. The jury awarded the plaintiff $1,800,000 in damages.

Having found the plaintiff to be 40 percent negligent and the OSAA 60 percent negligent, the damages assessed against the OSAA were reduced to $980,000 in accordance with the comparative fault doctrine embodied in the Oregon Tort Claims Act. The $100,000 out-of-court settlement with the district was subtracted from the $980,000 leaving the OSAA to pay $880,000.

The OSAA appealed charging that the filing of the suit against OSAA failed to meet the time requirements as set forth by the tort claims act, that it was not responsible for the school's actions, and that the award exceeded the $100,000 cap on liability as set forth by the tort claims act. The court upheld the lower court finding. It held that the suit was not time barred and that the OSAA did have responsibility for its failure to make safety recommendations to its member schools.

The court ruled that private organizations are not entitled to the $100,000 limited liability under the Oregon Tort Claims Act as the liability cap applies to public entities only.

Kain v. Rockridge Community Unit School District No. 300
453 N.E. 2d 118

Issue: Violation of mandatory number of practices
before competition rule

Level of Court: District Appellate Court
Date/State: 1983/Illinois
Decision: Defendant/Affirmed

The plaintiff brought suit against the school district and his high school football coach as a result of injuries he received during a game. The suit claimed the defendants were negligent in allowing him to play even though he had not participated in the minimum number of practice sessions required by Illinois High School Association rules. The trial court granted the defendant's motion to dismiss the case holding that the district and coach were acting in loco parentis and as such were not liable for ordinary negligence.

On appeal, the plaintiff argued that the immunity statute applies only to situations in which the teacher has discretion and since the IHSA rule prohibits playing football without adequate practice, the coach has no discretion and, therefore, the immunity statute was inapplicable.

The court ruled that the tort liability statute made no such distinction between discretionary and nondiscretionary acts. In upholding the lower court dismissal of the case, the Appellate Court ruled that the defendants were statutorily immune from suit.

Note. In jurisdictions not covered by immunity, courts have generally looked with disfavor at schools or school districts which violate their own adopted rules. If a rule is adopted for safety reasons, any violation of the rule is going to be very difficult to defend when a student or athlete injury occurs.

Leahy v. School Board of Hernando County
450 So. 2d 883

> Issue: Lack of special instructions for those
> without helmets in football drill

Level of Court: District Court of Appeals
Date/State: 1984/Florida
Decision: Defendant/Reversed and remanded

The plaintiff was one of several freshmen who did not receive a helmet when they were issued on the first day of practice because of the unavailability of the correct sizes. No special instructions were given by the football coaches to those who had not received helmets about any limitations on their participation in football practice. On the second day of practice all players took part in an agility drill. This drill involved having a dozen experienced players, with helmets on, get on their hands and knees and line up in a row. The remaining players were instructed to "go to each lineman, hit him on the shoulders with both hands, fall and roll on the ground, and then get back up to their feet as quickly as possible and move on to the next lineman." The drill was described as noncontact by the coaches although some contact clearly took place. The coaches supervised the drill from the sidelines. As the drill progressed, it became a little rougher with harder hitting and some people being knocked down. The plaintiff was the first player without a helmet to begin the drill. As his hands hit the lineman's shoulders as instructed, the lineman straightened his arms or raised his head and the plaintiff's face collided with his helmet. The plaintiff suffered facial injuries in addition to shattering his front teeth. The trial court awarded a directed verdict for the defendant and the plaintiff appealed.

On appeal, the plaintiff charged that the evidence supported four alleged acts of negligence on the part of the defendant and that the trial court, therefore, erred in granting a directed verdict for the defendant. The plaintiff alleged negligence in:

1. Failing to issue a helmet;
2. Failing to give any special instructions to those participating without helmets;

3. Allowing participation in a contact drill between players with helmets and players without helmets; and

4. Not limiting the intensity of participation involving those without helmets when it became apparent the drill was becoming aggressive.

The Appellate Court reversed the lower court decision and remanded the case for a new trial. The court ruled that the plaintiff had sufficiently argued a case of negligent supervision, as well as negligence in failing to provide adequate safety equipment, and should have been entitled to a jury determination based on the evidence.

Darrow v. West Genesee Central School District
342 N.Y.S. 2d 611

> Issue: Improper instruction — Insufficient safety instructions in soccer

Level of Court: Supreme Court, Appellate Division
Date/State: 1973/New York
Decision: Dismissed/Reversed

The plaintiff was injured while playing line soccer during his physical education class. The game was played by dividing the class into two teams and arranging them in opposing lines. The ball was centered between the two lines. Each team member was given a number with corresponding numbers being given to each of the players on the other team. The teacher called out one or more numbers and those whose numbers were called ran out and attempted to kick the ball through the opposing team's line.

The plaintiff alleged negligence in the teacher's failure to provide proper safety instructions. On the day of the accident, the plaintiff and another student ran into each other while going for the ball. By the teacher's own admission, he did not instruct the boys as to what they should do when two players met at the same time. Expert testimony indicated reasonable care required a demonstration and an explanation that students must play the ball as much as possible with their feet without charging to the ball to the point of bringing about bodily contact and without pushing and shoving.

The trial court dismissed the case without sending it to the jury. The Supreme Court reversed the dismissal and ordered a new trial. In reversing the dismissal, the Supreme Court held that teachers have an affirmative duty to instruct students in physical education classes on reasonable safety precautions to be observed while engaged in class activities. In noting the teacher's admission that he did not instruct the students as to what to do when two players met the ball at the same time, the court held there was sufficient evidence to warrant an examination and determination by the jury.

Alban v. Board of Education of Harford County
494 A. 2d 745

Issue: Improper placement and safeguards for
handicapped student in regular class

Level of Court: State Court of Appeals
Date/State: 1985/Maryland
Decision: Defendant/Affirmed

The plaintiff, an eighth-grade mentally handicapped student enrolled in a regular physical education class, received serious injuries when she attempted a maneuver on the Swedish box. The plaintiff's IEP called for placement in the regular physical education program. The parents of the injured student filed suit claiming the district was negligent in placing their daughter in the regular physical education class with no special safeguards to protect her from injury.

The trial court awarded a directed verdict for both the school district and the teacher. The court held that the IEP was designed to provide a combination of special education and regular classes and that once the IEP had been formulated and approved by the parents, the student was to be treated as a normal participant in the physical education class. The court further held that absent the exhaustion of administrative remedies (i.e., a due process hearing) provided by statute for challenging placements, the question of placement could not properly come before the court.

The Court of Appeals upheld the trial court while noting that the plaintiff, once part of the regular class, enjoyed the same remedies for injury sustained in class as did the rest of the students in class. The district and its teacher were obligated to meet the standard of reasonable care in the conduct of the physical education class. In their action, however, the parents only charged negligent classroom placement and not negligent conduct of the class.

Note. Physical educators would be well advised to keep all activities within the ability of individual students. Individualized instruction for all students, not just those on specific IEPs, is sound educational practice. If physical educators teach to the masses and have the same expectations for everyone in a given class, they leave themselves vulnerable in the event of an accident.

While the actual placement of the above student was improperly before the court, the appropriateness of a particular exercise for the individual student, and the standard of reasonable care on the part of the teacher, could certainly have been challenged.

Brown v. Quaker Valley School District
486 A. 2d 526

> Issue: Improper instruction — Failure to warn of
> risk in gymnastics

Level of Court: Commonwealth Court
Date/State: 1984/Pennsylvania
Decision: Defendant/Affirmed

Plaintiff was injured as a result of doing a straddle vault in her high school physical education class. She alleged negligence on the part of the instructor for failing to "adequately instruct and supervise gymnastic students as to the safe and proper method of using inherently dangerous equipment and failing to adequately warn her of the dangers posed by the use of such equipment."

The trial court granted the district's motion for summary judgment, holding the district not liable on the grounds of governmental immunity. On appeal, the Commonwealth Court upheld the governmental immunity of the school district and the physical educator.

Note. While the substantive issues of negligence were not entertained or discussed by the court because of the governmental immunity issue and decision, this case sounds a warning for a growing issue in physical education and sport. In any area of physical education or sport where the risk is elevated, such as in gymnastics and football, the instructions should include a clear warning of the *specific* risks involved in the activity. The failure to warn is increasingly being brought into negligence suits involving physical education and sport programs.

Becket v. Clinton Prairie School Corp.
504 N.E. 2d 552

Issue: Failure to warn and inadequate supervision— Collision of two baseball players

Level of Court: State Supreme Court
Date/State: 1987/Indiana
Decision: Defendant/Reversed and remanded/Reversed

The plaintiff, a senior on the baseball team, suffered a broken jaw as a result of a collision with another player during practice. Evidence indicated that the plaintiff, an outfielder, was injured during a drill conducted by the assistant coach. The coach acted as the hitter in this drill. Thirty yards in front of the coach was the cutoff man and 30 yards behind him was a line of outfielders. The coach would hit a fly ball to the outfielder at the end of the line who would then throw the ball to the cutoff man. The cutoff man would throw it to a shagger who stood off to the side of the coach.

After the coach hit the ball to the plaintiff, the plaintiff called for the ball. The coach called for the cutoff man to catch the ball. The wind was blowing hard and it was difficult for the players to hear the instructions. The cutoff man testified he was only to catch the ball upon instructions from the coach to do so. The cutoff man did not hear the plaintiff call for the ball and the plaintiff did not hear the coach call for the cutoff man to catch it. The two players collided head on and the plaintiff received his injuries. The plaintiff alleged that the coach:

"1. Failed to warn of the danger of the collision;
2. Failed to adequately supervise the practice;
3. Failed to post sufficient personnel to watch for possible collisions;
4. Conducted practice in an unreasonably dangerous manner; and
5. Allowed supervisory personnel to participate directly in the practice."

The trial court granted summary judgment for the defendant, holding the district did not breach its duty to the plaintiff. The Court of Appeals held that the district and the coaching staff owed the plaintiff a duty of care and that a dispute of material facts relative to a breach of this duty existed and, therefore, the case was a proper one for jury consideration and not summary judgment. It reversed the trial court decision and remanded the case for further proceedings.

On appeal to the Supreme Court, the defendants argued that the standard of care applied by the Court of Appeals was inappropriate. They argued that they should only be liable for willful and wanton behavior. Indiana law has held that school districts have a duty to exercise ordinary and reasonable care for the safety of children it oversees. The district argued that a less demanding standard of care should be required of school personnel supervising older children. The district further argued that the plaintiff assumed all ordinary inherent risks of playing baseball and that it should, therefore, be excused from the duty to use ordinary and reasonable care.

The Supreme Court ruled that as a matter of law, the district had the duty to use reasonable care and supervision. The question of whether the defendant exercised the duty with the level of care of an ordinary prudent person under the same or similar circumstances was a factual determination for the jury.

The court held, however, that trial court evidence clearly showed that the plaintiff had actual knowledge of the risk of collisions in baseball and had voluntarily incurred the risk as a participant. The Supreme Court ruled, therefore, that the defense of incurred risk was valid and the summary judgment of the trial court based on incurred risk proper.

Note. A distinction between interscholastic athletics and physical education needs to be emphasized here. Key to the assumption of risk defense is the voluntary assumption of a known and appreciated risk. While this defense can be sucessfully employed in the interscholastic sport setting in those jurisdictions allowing this defense, it is usually inapplicable in the elementary or secondary school physical education program. This is due to the fact that participation in the physical education class and participation in specific activities within the class are seldom voluntary.

Hedges v. Swan Lake and Salmon Prairie School District No. 73
812 P. 2d 334

Issue: Student struck by shot thrown by teacher

Level of Court: Supreme Court
Date/State: 1991/Montana
Decision: Defendant/Affirmed in part, reversed and
               remanded in part

The plaintiff, a 12-year-old elementary school student, was injured when struck by a shot that was thrown by her teacher. The plaintiff had been directed by her teacher to mark where her shots landed. She was marking a previous throw when struck by another shot thrown by the teacher. By statute, school districts and their employees are immune to liability for negligence in Montana. The trial court granted summary judgment for both the defendant teacher and defendant school district.

On appeal, the summary judgment for the teacher was upheld. The judgment for the school district was reversed, however, as the court found that the purchase of liability insurance by the district waived its immunity to the extent of its insurance coverage. The case against the district was remanded to the trial court for further proceedings and determination.

Note. The issue considered and discussed by the Appellate Court in this case was the impact of purchasing liability insurance on the immunity granted to school districts by statute. Physical educators and coaches need to focus closely on the activity itself. Numerous accidents involving the shot put occur each year. Discussions by the authors with teaching and coaching peers reveal a significant number of near misses in class and team participation in both the shot put and discus throw. Because of the potential deadly consequences of mishaps in these activities, it is imperative that carefully planned and communicated procedures for the teaching and supervision of these activities be developed at the building level.

Step-by-step procedures and expectations need to be developed which clearly establish the responsibilities of the instructor, the thrower, the retriever, the measurer, and the spectator. Expectations and safety precautions need to be repeated often, and clear warnings about the potential consequences of injury need to be presented to students. It is not enough to communicate and repeat procedural and behavioral expectations. Established expectations need to be consistently enforced.

Brod v. Central School District No. 1
386 N.Y.S. 2d 125

Issue: Improper instructions — Going barefoot in the gym

Level of Court: Supreme Court, Appellate Divison
Date/State: 1976/New York
Decision: Plaintiff/Amended re: damages

The plaintiff, a nine-year-old student, was instructed by his physical education teacher to go barefoot if he wanted to participate in class, as a result of forgetting his gym shoes. While chasing a ball in class, the plaintiff's feet stuck to the floor causing him to lose his balance and fall. As a result of the fall, he lost two front teeth. The jury returned a verdict for the plaintiff awarding him $15,000 and $3,800 to his father.

On appeal, the Supreme Court affirmed the lower court finding of negligence, stating the evidence supported a finding of negligent instruction and that the negligent instruction was the proximate cause of the plaintiff's injuries. The Supreme Court ruled that the trial court was in error in instructing the jury that lawyer's fees are customarily paid from jury verdicts and ordered a new trial limited to the issue of damages.

Note: Going barefoot during physical education class is not an acceptable practice (neither is the dangerous alternative of participating in stocking feet). When students come to class without the proper shoes or attire that would allow for their safe participation in the class activity, they should either have their activity for the day modified or be excluded from participation.

IN SUMMARY

THE REASONABLY PRUDENT PHYSICAL EDUCATOR OR COACH:

1. Develops written unit plans for each unit of study or sport season to ensure that proper progressions and safety are built into each activity unit.

2. Develops daily, written lesson plans which allow for adequate warm-up, instruction and practice with both classroom management and safety considerations included.

3. Analyzes his/her teaching or coaching methods not only for their effectiveness but for their attention to student and athlete safety.

4. Provides adequate instruction before requiring student or athlete participation in any activity, including verbal instructions as well as teacher and/or student demonstrations.

5. Provides adequate safety instructions prior to any activity.

6. Provides clear warnings to students and athletes as to the specific risks involved in any activity or in the use of equipment, facilities or grounds.

Continued

7. Teaches or coaches only those activities with which he/she is familiar and qualified to teach/coach.

8. Gives proper instructions for both skill and safety which conform to recognized standards employed in the professional field.

9. Does not coerce students to perform.

10. Selects activities which are appropriate for the age of student being instructed and is familiar with any existing district or state scope and sequence documents.

11. Follows all guidelines related to program which are set forth by the school, district, state, or activity association.

12. Requires an adequate amount of practice before competition.

13. Does not attempt to instruct or supervise an excessive number of students or athletes, especially in activities involving elevated levels of risk.

14. Continues to upgrade both skill and knowledge through participation in workshops, continuing education and other inservice opportunities.

SUPERVISION

More claims are filed against teachers and coaches for improper supervision than for any other single reason. The supervisory duties of physical education and sport personnel are many and require more than mere presence or passive supervision.

While absence from one's class or team does not constitute negligence as a matter of law, courts have pretty much agreed that it is reasonable to expect teachers and coaches to be present in classes and practice sessions which they have been entrusted to teach or coach. Decisions on negligence due to temporary absence from the classroom have gone both ways. In determining whether or not temporary absence on the part of a teacher or coach constitutes negligence, the courts generally examine the equipment with which, and the activity in which, the students or athletes are working as well as the age and composition of the group, the instructor's past experience with the group and the reason and duration of the teacher's or coach's absence.

In addition to presence in the classroom or activity area, the supervisory duties of physical education and sport staff generally include passage to and from the activity, locker room and hall supervision. Case law has made it abundantly clear that teachers and coaches are expected to be where assigned on time and to provide active rather than passive supervision.

Active supervision requires more than mere presence. In addition to overseeing student participation in the assigned activity, physical education and sport personnel are expected to monitor and keep activities within the skill level of individual students and athletes; keep them from participating in dangerous and unsafe activities; enforce class, team, and school rules; keep records and be aware of the health status of individual students and athletes; make accommodations for size, age and skill differences when matching students for participation or competition; and provide spotting and other specific supervision in activities of elevated risk, such as gymnastics, wrestling and football.

The skill level within the average physical education class varies greatly from student to student. Depending upon the activity, it may or may not be reasonable to expect all students to perform at the same level or even perform the same task. Individualization of instruction not only makes good sense educationally, but also makes for good practice from a liability standpoint. It is one way to help staff effectively monitor individual student progress and to assure that instructional demands are within the skill capability of the individual student. In the athletic setting, this is somewhat taken care of as athletes are ability grouped and placed on either a frosh, JV or varsity roster.

Students, especially younger ones, do not always display the best judgment in their activity with peers. Physical education and sport staff, through their efforts of supervision, need to guard against students and athletes participating in dangerous and unsafe activities. In the physical education and sport setting, this becomes especially important in the moments before class or practice actually starts as students begin to assemble in the gymnasium or on the practice field. Horseplay is not a harmless passage of time and these moments before the start of class or practice cannot be "down time" for the teacher or coach. In guarding against unsafe and dangerous activities, physical education and sport personnel also have to be alert to those students, who for one reason or another, are determined to perform or attempt skills which are beyond their capability.

Reasonable classroom, team and schoolwide rules are a necessity for the efficient and safe operation of school programs. This is especially true for the physical education and sport setting due to the nature of the activities and the equipment and facilities used to carry out the programs. Courts have not been very understanding of schools and staff when these established rules have not been enforced. The message sent by the courts is clear. Schools and staff are not free to violate or fail to enforce their own rules. To do so has been held to constitute negligent behavior.

Student discipline is an important element in all school programs. Effective, productive and appropriate measures for student discipline need to be established. The use of corporal punishment makes physical educators and coaches vulnerable to litigation and should be avoided. This includes the prescription of exercise such as laps and push-ups for discipline or punishment purposes.

Being aware of the health status of the students in a class or on a team is a critical responsibility of physical educators and coaches. A number of permanent and temporary conditions can affect a student or athlete's ability to fully participate in the activities within the given program. It is clearly within the responsibility of the physical educator or coach to be aware of any conditions which might preclude an individual student or athlete from fully participating in a given activity as well as being aware of those conditions which might require first aid and prompt attention. Physical education and sport staff would be well advised to be aware of all students in their classes or on their teams who have medical conditions such as seizure disorders, bee sting allergies, severe asthma, or any other condition which might require prompt action on their part in a crisis situation.

It is also imperative that teachers and coaches keep files on students and athletes who have brought in medical excuses for temporary exclusion from given activities. Any student who is removed from participation by doctor's note should only be readmitted with the doctor's written permission. Physical education and sport personnel need to be aware of the reason for any extended absence of a student and, where necessary for health and safety reasons, their return to activity should be gradual and modified.

Even though with certain students it 's a temptation to do so, excuses from home or from the student relative to their inability to participate should not be dismissed lightly. It is a much safer policy to honor the excuse for that day and follow up with the home in those cases where the teacher or coach suspects a problem other than health. The courts will not view favorably any attempts by physical education or sport personnel to diagnose possible medical problems.

Although much more so at some grade levels than others, each physical education class is characterized by variances in size, experience and, in some cases, age. These variances can be extreme in some instances. It is the responsibility of the physical educator or coach to make accommodations for these variances when matching students up for general participation as well as competition. While this is often attended to in individual activities such as combatives, it is equally neglected in a good number of others. Accommodations should be made whenever there is a foreseeable risk of physical contact of any type. Again, in the athletic setting, this is somewhat accomplished by the ability grouping which is inherent to the forming of athletic teams. Some care still needs to be taken, however, to avoid significant mismatches.

The courts, while being very clear about the required duty of teachers and coaches to provide active supervision, have been equally clear in holding that they are not insurers of student safety and that proper supervision does not necessarily require constant and continuous sight of all students by supervising teachers and coaches. The nature of the activities as well as the age, capacity, experience, and number of participants play a role in determining the extent of supervision required.

The following cases are offered as further illustration of how the courts view the critical issue of supervision.

Dailey v. Los Angeles Unified School District
470 P. 2d 360

Issue: Inadequate supervision — Failure to actively
supervise in assigned area of responsibility

Level of Court: State Supreme Court
Date/State: 1970/California
Decision: Defendant/Affirmed/Reversed

Parents of a deceased high school student brought a wrongful death suit against two physical education teachers and the school district as a result of a "slapboxing" match which occurred outside of the gym during the lunch hour. The trial court directed a verdict in favor of the teachers and school district and the directed verdict was affirmed by the Appellate Court.

Testimony showed that the two boys approached the gym during their lunch hour, as their next class was physical education. They stopped outside of the gym and engaged in "slapboxing," a form of boxing using open hands rather than fists. The activity was in fun. The plaintiff's son fell backward during the course of the activity and fractured his skull. He died a few hours later.

The parents claimed the school was negligent in its supervision during the lunch hour. Testimony indicated that according to the building plan, the physical education department had responsibility for the general supervision of the gym area. The department chair, one of the defendants, testified that although the physical education department had supervision duty for the gym area, he had never been told to have a duty roster assigning particular teachers supervision duty on particular days. He testified there was a teacher on duty in the gym office on the day of the accident. The teacher on duty was eating lunch and doing lesson plans. He was not in a position to observe the accident.

The trial court issued a directed verdict for the defendants which required that the evidence, in the light most favorable to the plaintiff, be insufficient to draw any inference of negligence in support of the plaintiff's claims. The Court of Appeals upheld the directed verdict.

On appeal, the Supreme Court first looked at the duty owed by school districts to students on school grounds. They held that California law had long imposed a duty to supervise the conduct of children on school grounds at all times and to enforce the rules and regulations designed for their protection. The court noted that lack of supervision or ineffective supervision under California law could constitute a lack of ordinary care on the part of those responsible for supervision.

The court further noted that the student's death, as a result of his own conduct would not preclude a finding of negligence on the part of the school district, as adolescents are not adults and should not be expected to exercise the same degree of discretion and judgment as an adult.

The court ruled that, in light of the building plan assigning general supervision responsibility to the physical education department for the gym area, there was evidence that the department had neglected to develop a supervision duty schedule. There was evidence that the department head had failed to instruct his subordinates on what was expected of them relative to their supervision responsibilities. There was also evidence that the teacher on duty the day of the accident did not supervise at all but rather ate lunch, talked on the phone and did lesson plans. The court noted that neither of the two teachers named as defendants heard or saw anything the day of the accident despite the testimony indicating the activity attracted a crowd of 20-30 people.

Based on the above, the Supreme Court held that there was sufficient evidence from which a jury could conclude that those charged with supervision were negligent in exercising due care in the performance of their duties. The Supreme Court reversed the directed verdict.

Sheehan v. St. Peter's Catholic School
188 N.W. 2d 868

Issue: Improper supervision — Teacher absent
from playground

Level of Court: State Supreme Court
Date/State: 1971/Minnesota
Decision: Plaintiff/Affirmed

The plaintiff, an eighth grade student, was one of 20 girls escorted to an athletic field by their teacher for morning recess. They were directed to sit on a log along the third base line of a baseball field being used by eighth grade boys. The teacher returned to the school building and did not return until after the accident.

Testimony indicated that about five minutes after the teacher left, some of the boys who were waiting to bat began throwing pebbles at the girls. This lasted three to four minutes despite the protests of the girls. As a result of the pebble throwing, the plaintiff was struck in the eye and ended up losing sight in that eye. The plaintiff filed suit on the basis of inadequate supervision and the trial court awarded for the plaintiff. The defendant appealed, asserting a defense of contributory negligence.

The Supreme Court ruled the assertion of contributory negligence at the time of the appeal was improper as no claim to this effect was made during the two years which passed from the accident up to and including the trial from which the appeal originated. In upholding the trial court's finding of negligence for improper supervision, the court ruled that while the school district was not an insurer of student safety, it was required to exercise reasonable and ordinary care in supervision of students. The Court noted that the courts have not required constant and continuous supervision of every student and have not found defendants negligent, in the temporary absence of supervision, where the inflicted injuries were sudden and without warning and where they occurred in such a manner that supervision would not have prevented them. The Supreme Court held that this was not the case here, as the pebble throwing occurred over a 3–4 minute period of time before the injury was inflicted and the presence of the teacher presumably would have put an end to the activity. The Supreme Court upheld the finding for the plaintiff.

Cirillo v. City of Milwaukie
150 N.W. 2d 460

Issue: Inadequate supervision — Teacher absent from gym

Level of Court: State Supreme Court
Date/State: 1967/Wisconsin
Decision: Defendant/Reversed

The plaintiff, a 14-year-old high school student, was injured during a game of keep-away in his physical education class while the physical education teacher was absent. Suit was brought against the defendant alleging negligence in failing to provide rules to guide the class, attempting to teach an excessive number of students and absenting himself from the gymnasium.

Trial court evidence showed that after taking roll, the teacher threw out some basketballs and told the 49 boys in the class to shoot around. The teacher left the class unsupervised at this point. Before long, a game of keep-away developed which became increasingly rowdy with running, pushing and tripping occurring all over the floor. It was during this "game" that the plaintiff fell and sustained injury. The teacher was absent from the class for 25 minutes. The defendant denied negligence and alleged contributory negligence on the part of the plaintiff for failing to follow directions and in knowingly participating in the rowdy game in the gym. The defendant asked for and received a summary judgment and the plaintiff appealed.

The Supreme Court noted that the state summary judgment statute only allowed summary judgment for a defendant if the defendant's affidavit presents evidentiary facts that show that his defense is sufficient to defeat the plaintiff. It further stated that, as a drastic remedy, summary judgment should only be used where there is no substantial issue of fact or inferences to be drawn from the facts. The Supreme Court concluded there were substantial issues of fact in question and, as such, were proper for jury consideration. The court held that a jury might find negligence in the teacher's extended absence from the class. The court said, "It does not seem inherently unreasonable to expect that teachers will be present in classes which they are entrusted to teach." The court was careful to note, however, that the absence of a teacher does not constitute negligence as a matter of law. The teacher's duty is to use reasonable care. In determining whether a teacher's absence represents a breach of reasonable care, the court suggested a number of factors may bear on this determination, including:

1. "The activity in which the students are engaged;
2. The instrumentalities with which the students are working;
3. The age and composition of the class;
4. Past experience with the class; and
5. The reason for and duration of the teacher's absence."

The court ruled that only in rare cases is it permissible for a court to hold as a matter of law that the negligence of one party constitutes at least 50 percent of the total and that the apportionment of negligence is almost always for the jury. The court recognized that the ages of the respective parties were an important consideration when apportioning negligence.

The defendant claimed to permit recovery for the plaintiff would be to "constitute the defendant an insurer of the safety of Milwaukie school children." This belief was supported by the trial court. The Supreme Court explained that while it recognized that a teacher is neither immune from liability nor an insurer of student safety, he/she is liable for any failure to use reasonable care and to permit recovery where a defendant was negligent was not equivalent to rendering the defendant an insurer of student safety. The Supreme Court reversed the summary judgment for the defendants.

Leger v. Stockton Unified School District
249 Cal. Rptr. 688

Issue: Lack of supervision — Wrestler assaulted while dressing in unsupervised restroom

Level of Court: Court of Appeals
Date/State: 1988/California
Decision: Defendant/Reversed

The plaintiff, a member of the JV wrestling team, was assaulted by a nonstudent in an unsupervised restroom as he was changing clothes before practice. The restroom was used by a number of team members to change. As a result of injuries received in the assault, the plaintiff brought suit against the school district claiming:

1. A violation of his inalienable right to attend a safe school under the California State Constitution;
2. A breach of the defendants' constitutional duty to make the school safe; and
3. A breach of their legal duty to provide adequate supervision.

The trial court sustained the demurrer of the school district. A general demurrer is an allegation of a defendant which admits the facts alleged by the complaint to be true yet insufficient for the plaintiff to proceed upon or to oblige the defendant to answer.

The Appellate Court reversed the lower court decision. The court held that while the State Constitutional provisions cited by the plaintiff did not provide for the right to sue for damages, school authorities did in fact owe the student a duty of care and were not immune from liability under statutory provisions of tort law. The court therefore concluded that the trial court erred when it sustained the defendant's general demurrer to the plaintiff's complaint.

Childress v. Madison County
777 S.W. 2d 1

Issue: Supervision and liability release — Mentally retarded
student in swimming

Level of Court: Court of Appeals
Date/State: 1989/Tennessee
Decision: Defendant/Affirmed in part, reversed in part
               and remanded

The plaintiff, a 20-year-old severely retarded student, traveled with his high school class to the YMCA to train for the Special Olympics. He was supervised on this trip by a teacher and an aide who were employees of the county and by a YMCA lifeguard. The plaintiff's event consisted of walking the width of the shallow end of the pool and handing a floating ball to an attendant. The teacher was at the shallow end, the aide at the other end, and the lifeguard was in and out of the pool while giving instructions. On the day of the accident, the teacher had finished working with the plaintiff and instructed him, as well as all of the other children to get out of the pool. As the students were exiting the pool, another student, who was a swimmer, jumped in to swim a lap. The teacher walked along the edge as he swam to the deep end.

The next time the plaintiff was seen he was lying on the floor of the pool where it slopes from the shallow end to the deep end. He was pulled from the pool and revived by the lifeguard. As a result of the accident, the plaintiff sustained injuries and incurred medical expenses. The case was tried before the court without a jury. The court ruled the evidence did not weigh in favor of the plaintiff and held for the defendants.

On appeal, the court of appeals ruled that the evidence preponderated against a finding of no negligence. The court held that the teacher and the aide were responsible for supervision, that the teacher ordered students out of the pool but did not actually see the plaintiff exit, that the teacher became involved in observing another student and did not know whether the plaintiff left the pool, and that the teacher did not know whether anyone else was watching the plaintiff when she left him. The court took note that each of the attendants was involved in small group instruction and no one had responsibility for general supervision of the entire group. The court held that general supervision could have prevented the accident.

The defendants raised the fact that the mother had signed a liability release removing all liability from the defendants. The court ruled that the release was valid as far as the mother's claims were concerned but that the mother could not execute a valid release or exculpatory clause on behalf of her son. The court, in ruling the release invalid, held that guardians may not waive the rights of their children or those of incompetents.

It was also recognized that releases are contracts and that minors and incompetents cannot legally execute a contract. The Court of Appeals reversed and remanded the case as it pertains to the boy. The case by the mother individually was dismissed.

Weber v. Yeo
383 N.W. 2d 230

Issue: Improper supervision — Swimming class

Level of Court: State Court of Appeals
Date/State: 1985/Michigan
Decision: Defendant/Reversed in part

A wrongful death suit was brought on behalf of a student who drowned while enrolled in a middle school swimming class. The suit was filed against all three swimming instructors, the school administrators and the school district. The student had dived into the deep end of the pool and failed to resurface. He was pulled from the pool but all attempts to revive him failed. The plaintiff alleged negligence of the instructors and school district for:

1. Improperly removing the victim from the pool;
2. Improperly carrying out resuscitative efforts;
3. Not properly observing each student in the class;
4. Not properly positioning themselves around the pool;
5. Not immediately providing assistance and first aid;
6. Not refraining from activities which would distract their attention from their supervisory responsibilities; and
7. Failing to warn parents of the condition of the pool, the lack of a lifeguard, and the lack of constant supervision of those in the class.

The trial court granted a summary judgment for all of the defendants while holding that their actions were discretionary and therefore cloaked in governmental immunity. The Court of Apppeals ruled that, while the manner of rescue from the pool was discretionary, the resuscitative efforts, instruction, supervision, and failure to warn all constituted ministerial acts for which the defendants did not enjoy immunity. The Appellate Court reversed the summary judgment pertaining to the above ministerial acts, ruling they were proper questions for the jury.

Smith v. Vernon Parish School Board
442 So. 2d 1319

Issue: Supervision — Students violate rules pertaining to
use of a trampoline

Level of Court: Court of Appeals
Date/State: 1983/Louisiana
Decision: Defendant/Affirmed

A 15-year-old girl broke an arm and a wrist as a result of a fall on a trampoline during her physical education class. The plaintiff brought suit against the school board, physical education teacher and the insurer of the teacher claiming negligent supervision. Evidence showed that plaintiff's daughter was a straight A student with four years of instruction in the use of trampolines. On the day of the accident, she and four other girls requested permission to bounce on the trampoline which was stored on the stage in the gymnasium. The physical education teacher helped the girls open the trampoline, watched them for a couple of minutes, then left the stage to talk to another teacher who was teaching a class in the gym. Testimony showed that after the physical education teacher left the stage, the girls sent a friend to make sure the teacher could not see them and then all five girls proceeded to bounce on the trampoline at the same time. After one bounce, all five fell on the bed of the trampoline and the injury resulted. Testimony was clear that the physical education teacher had a steadfast rule of no more than two people on the trampoline at a time, that this rule had been repeated to the class on numerous occasions, and that the safety hazard of having more than two on at a time was made clear to all members of the class.

The trial court found the physical education teacher free of negligence and the plaintiff's daughter contributorily negligent in causing her own injuries and, therefore, awarded no damages. The plaintiff appealed the trial court decision to the Court of Appeals.

The Court of Appeals reiterated that the duties of teachers required the exercise of reasonable supervision, commensurate with the age of the children and the circumstances, and that a greater degree of care must be exercised only when requiring students to use objects which are inherently dangerous or where it can be reasonably foreseen that an injury or accident will occur. The court affirmed the lower court decision that the teacher, under the circumstances, exercised reasonable care and that the "greater degree of care standard" did not apply in this case because the trampoline was not an inherently dangerous object and had the rules been followed, the activity was not one where it was reasonably foreseeable that an accident might occur. The court stated that the girl "by a conscious and willful violation of the rules, cannot transform a non-risky event into one in which the accident is reasonably foreseeable." Because of finding no negligence on the part of the defendants, the court did not discuss or rule on the issue of contributory negligence on behalf of the plaintiff's daughter.

Crowell v. School District No. 7 of Gallatin County
805 P. 2d 522

Issue: Supervision and spotting in gymnastics class

Level of Court: Supreme Court
Date/State: 1991/Montana
Decision: Defendant/Reversed and remanded

The plaintiff was injured in her physical education class while performing a gymnastics routine on the rings. Testimony indicated that students were required to perform compulsory exercises on the parallel bars, high bar, rings, balance beam, and vault. The class was divided into several small groups which rotated through the various equipment stations.

On the day of her injury, the plaintiff was attempting a straddle-cut dismount from the rings. The plaintiff failed to generate enough momentum and as her legs swung overhead and around the rings, she released and dropped to the floor landing on her shoulders and neck rather than rotating around to her feet. Testimony indicated that the plaintiff was not being directly supervised at the time of the injury. The teacher did not spot the plaintiff through the dismount and although students were assigned responsibility for spotting one another, no one spotted the plaintiff as she attempted the dismount.

The district filed for summary judgment to dismiss the case claiming both the district and the teacher were immune to suit by state statute. The trial court granted the request for summary judgment and the plaintiff appealed. On appeal, the plaintiff argued that even if the defendants were immune by statute, that immunity was waived as a result of the district's purchase of liability insurance. The Appellate Court ruled that while the district and its employees were immune by statute, that immunity was waived to the extent of their insurance coverage. The case was remanded to the trial court for further proceedings.

Note. While this case centered on immunity and the impact of purchasing liability insurance on that immunity, it nonetheless sounds a clear warning to physical educators. Gymnastics is an activity characterized by more risk than many parts of the physical education curriculum; therefore it demands very close attention to the duty of supervision. Care needs to be given when setting up gymnastics stations, in a class situation, to avoid multiple "high risk" activities. It is essential that proper spotting be provided for all aerial activities such as the one being performed by the plaintiff in this case.

If a physical educator or coach elects to have students spot one another, it is crucial that those student spotters receive careful instruction on proper spotting technique and that they undergo adequate and well-supervised practice on those spotting techniques. The teacher retains the ultimate responsibility for the supervision of all spotters as well as other class members. Delegating responsibility for spotting to students is an action which should be undertaken very carefully.

It would be prudent for physical educators to carefully plan their gymnastics units to avoid situations where multiple high risk activities are occurring simultaneously in different areas of the gym. For example, if one station has students performing a routine on the rings with an aerial dismount, the teacher might be wise to plan isolated and more controlled skill work on the remaining pieces of equipment. This would allow closer supervision of the "higher risk" station. Supervisors need to guard against spreading themselves too thin as well as guard against careless delegation of their supervisory responsibilities, including spotting, to others. The skill level and past experience of the participants plays an obvious role in making these decisions.

Barrera v. Dade County School Board
366 So. 2d 531

Issue: Adequate supervision in gymnastics class
employing stations

Level of Court: District Court of Appeals
Date/State: 1979/Florida
Decision: Defendant/Reversed and remanded

The plaintiff, an 8-year-old third grade student, was injured during her physical education class when another student was pushed off a balance beam by a girl who had previously displayed rowdy behavior. The pushed girl fell onto the plaintiff's leg and broke it. Evidence at trial established that the elementary school gymnastics class had 30 students and was under the supervision of one physical education teacher. At the time of the accident, the class was divided into three equal groups with one group working on tumbling, one working on the parallel bars, and one working on balance beam. The teacher did not see the accident occur as she was helping a girl at the parallel bars.

The trial court granted the defendants motion for summary judgment, holding the evidence clearly weighed in favor of the defendant. The Court of Appeals reversed the lower court ruling while holding that the defendant had not conclusively demonstrated that, under the circumstances, it had provided adequate supervision for the class. The court ruled that the question of negligence in this case was clearly a question for the jury and not proper for summary judgment. The case was remanded for a jury trial.

Note. The use of multiple stations in physical education classes is common and can create a motivating and active learning environment. Care needs to be taken when employing stations, however, to ensure that supervision is adequate. If only one teacher is present, it would be prudent to have no more than one station where the risk is substantially elevated. When supervising multiple stations, it is imperative that physical educators position themselves in a manner which allows them to provide specific supervision or spotting at a station where the risk is elevated, such as the parallel bars, while maintaining general supervision of the remainder of the class.

Marlowe v. Rush-Henrietta Central School District
578 N.Y.S. 2d 872

Issue: Poor supervision — Bat thrown by student

Level of Court: Court of Appeals
Date/State: 1991/New York
Decision: Plaintiff/Reversed with dissent

The plaintiff, a 17-year-old high school student, was struck in the face and mouth by a bat while playing in a baseball game. The game took place during a physical education class which the plaintiff voluntarily joined during his noon recess. Evidence indicated the bat was thrown at least 35 feet by another student, that this student had a reputation of throwing the bat and that school officials did little or nothing to enforce the safety rules of the game or to instruct the offending student in proper conduct. Suit was filed against the student who threw the bat as well as the school district.

The defendants filed a motion for summary judgment which the trial court denied. On appeal, the Supreme Court, Appellate Division, ruled that the plaintiff assumed the risk of being hit by a bat when he joined the game and that no allegation was made that the bat was intentionally thrown. The Appellate Court concluded that the trial court erred in not granting the summary judgment for the defendants and, therefore, reversed the lower court ruling thereby dismissing the case.

Two members of the Appellate Court submitted a dissenting opinion. In their dissent, they held that a participant in a sport activity assumes only those risks which are "known, apparent, or reasonably foreseeable." They further stated that the issue of risk assumption is a factual question to be answered by jury determination. They note that in the case at hand, the plaintiff was aware that bats were occasionally thrown in baseball games and that the student defendant had a history of throwing the bat. However, evidence clearly indicated that he had never seen a bat thrown the distance which occurred in this case. In their opinion, a question existed as to whether the risk was apparent or reasonably foreseeable. The dissent also makes note of the fact that the student defendant admitted that the bat did not slip but that he had, in fact, simply let it go in clear violation of the rules of the game. The dissent concludes that a triable issue existed relative to whether the student's conduct was reckless or wanton which would preclude a summary judgment. Finally, the dissent notes that the apparent failure of the school district to adequately enforce the safety rules or to instruct the student defendant in proper conduct presents a jury question as to whether or not the school's actions constituted a breach of their duty of care. The decision was affirmed by the Court of Appeals.

Note. Physical educators and coaches would be wise to focus on the dissenting opinion in this case. It is critically important not only to communicate reasonable safety rules and expectations but to consistently enforce them. Any reckless behavior by class or team members needs to be recognized and attended to by the supervisor of the activity. Failure to do so implies approval of the behavior and would certainly open up the question of duty and breach of duty to close examination.

Clark v. Furch
567 S.W. 2d 457

Issue: Supervision — Free time on playground

Level of Court: State Court of Appeals
Date/State: 1978/Missouri
Decision: Defendant/Affirmed

A six-year-old kindergarten student broke his arm during his physical education class as a result of swinging by a jump rope tied to a jungle gym. The parents brought suit, on behalf of their son, against the physical education teacher alleging negligent supervision.

The evidence showed that the plaintiff and the other 21 members of his kindergarten physical education class had been jumping rope on the playground pursuant to the teacher's instructions. Near the end of the 20 minute class period, the students were given free time to play on the swings, slide and jungle gym. The plaintiff, still in possession of the jump rope, climbed to the top of the jungle gym, tied the rope to the top bar and started to swing down. As a result, he fell and broke his arm.

Testimony indicated the plaintiff had been taught for almost an entire semester about the use of the playground equipment and was aware that his action was dangerous. At the time the plaintiff climbed up the apparatus, the teacher was looking in a direction away from him. The evidence gave no indication of how long it took the boy to go from the ground to the top of the apparatus or how long he was there before he fell. No evidence suggested the teacher was inattentive or saw the boy climbing the apparatus with the rope in his hand.

The trial court entered judgment in favor of the teacher and the plaintiff appealed. On appeal, the plaintiff challenged the admission of the evidence on contributory negligence as a six-year-old is incapable of contributory negligence as a matter of law. The Court of Appeals upheld the finding of the lower court ruling that no evidence of negligence was apparent. The court stated the teacher's duty was to exercise ordinary care in supervising children. The teacher is not an insurer of their safety. The court held that ordinary care does not require having each of the 22 six-year-olds constantly and continuously in sight. The court stated there was no indication that the teacher saw the boy in a place of danger or acting dangerously and failed to act; therefore there was an insufficent basis for liability.

Cook v. Bennett
288 N.W. 2d 609

> Issue: Improper supervision — Allowing students to play a hazardous game

Level of Court: Court of Appeals
Date/State: 1979/Michigan
Decision: Defendant/Affirmed in part, reversed in part

Plaintiffs, on behalf of their son, filed suit against the school principal and classroom teacher for injuries received by their elementary school son in the game "kill" being played during a recess period. The game "kill" consisted of one person having possession of a football while all other participants attempted to gain possession by tackling the person with the ball and wrestling it away.

Testimony indicated the game in question was ultra hazardous yet was allowed to be played on numerous occasions by both the teacher and the principal who observed it being played but made no attempt to stop it. On the day of the injury, the teacher was on leave of absence and was replaced by a substitute.

The teacher requested and received summary judgment in his favor stating that due to his absence, he owed no duty to supervise. The court issued summary judgment in favor of the principal as well on the basis of governmental immunity.

On appeal, the Court of Appeals upheld the summary judgment for the teacher and reversed the judgment for the principal. The Appellate Court ruled that the trial court erred in assigning governmental immunity to the actions of the principal. The court ruled that the principal's duty to supervise staff and students fell within her ministerial rather than discretionary powers. As a ministerial function, liability of the principal for supervision exists under Michigan law.

Note. This case raises a potentially important point for physical educators. The court, in this case, ruled that a teacher owes a duty of reasonable care over students in his or her charge and that this duty is coterminous with the teacher's presence at school as supervision implies oversight. It could be a mistake to assume that a teacher's absence automatically relieves the teacher of all duty. While certainly true, given the above set of facts, other factual circumstances could make the teacher's duty while absent an arguable point.

The fact that teachers have a professional duty, and in many districts, a duty imposed by board policy, to prepare lesson plans for the substitute, seems to imply that some duty remains. This duty might conceivably be linked to proper instruction and progressions as well as alerting substitutes to students with particular health problems and those students with a propensity toward disruption. Substitutes must be able to rely on being in a position to anticipate and foresee potential problems. Without adequate plans left by the regular teacher, this could become impossible in many circumstances.

Tashian v. North Colonie Central School District No. 5
375 N.Y.S. 2d 467

> Issue: Inadequate supervision — Failure to enforce school rules

Level of Court: State Supreme Court, Appellate Division
Date/State: 1975/New York
Decision: Plaintiff/Affirmed

A third grade student was injured during a softball game at lunch recess. He was hit on the nose by a baseball bat being swung by a fourth grade student. The student was given first aid and x-rays disclosed no broken bones. About four weeks after sustaining the injury, the student had an epileptic seizure followed by recurrent seizures thereafter. The boy required hospitalization and continued use of anti-convulsant medication.

The boy's parents brought suit alleging negligence in supervision on the part of the school district. The school regulations prohibited third graders from participating in softball games, although it was permissible for fourth graders to do so. Two supervisors were on duty that day but neither saw the accident. The trial court awarded $37,100 in damages and the district appealed.

In upholding the trial court decision in favor of the plaintiff, the Supreme Court held that there was a clear duty on the part of school districts to provide supervision of playground activities. In that there were regulations prohibiting third graders from playing softball at noontime, the court ruled that the district's failure to enforce its own rules constituted negligence and this negligence was the legal cause of the injury to the plaintiff's son.

Barrett v. Phillips
233 S.E. 2d 918

> Issue: Violation of state high school athletic association
> rules regarding ages and eligiblity

Level of Court: Court of Appeals
Date/State: 1976/North Carolina
Decision: Defendant/Affirmed

The plaintiff brought a wrongful death suit as the administrator of his son's estate when his son died after colliding with an opposing player during a high school football game. The plaintiff charged negligence in allowing a 20-year-old student to compete in violation of both North Carolina High School Athletic Association and North Carolina State Department of Public Instruction rules. The trial court granted the defendants' motion for summary judgment. The Court of Appeals upheld the lower court ruling while holding that even if the defendant violated the rules by letting the 20-year-old student participate, the violation of the rules was not the proximate cause of death.

Note. This case might have had a different outcome had the plaintiff adequately pleaded a mismatch for competetion. To prove a mismatch, however, requires more than a mere difference in age. Other pertinent factors would include size, skill, and experience.

Hopwood v. Elmwood Community High School District
525 N.E. 2d 247

Issue: Physical limitations on activity

Level of Court: District Court of Appeals
Date/State: 1988/Illinois
Decision: Defendant/Affirmed

The plaintiff, a 16-year-old high school student, injured her knee while playing a game of soccer in her physical education class. The suit alleged that the physical education teacher recklessly disregarded the plaintiff's safety by requiring her to participate in physical education while aware of her limitations and that administrative personnel failed to properly forward doctor's notes that limited her activity.

A year prior to the injury, the plaintiff claimed she submitted a letter from her doctor to her former physical education instructor which precluded her from participation in class for two weeks and thereafter allowed such activity as she was able to tolerate due to a knee injury. The plaintiff testified she informed her current physical education teacher of the prior injury as well as the letter from her doctor. The instructor requested the plaintiff to provide her with a written excuse from her mother, which she did on three separate occasions. The plaintiff indicated to the instructor that certain exercises caused her pain. After receiving the notes from home, the plaintiff was not required to perform those exercises.

On the day of the activity, the plaintiff did not complain of any difficulty with the activity being engaged in. She had played the game before. A group of girls became bored with the activity and stopped participating. The instructor threatened the group with disciplinary action if they failed to participate. The plaintiff continued to participate and never indicated to the instructor that her knee bothered her. During the course of the game, she fell and re-injured the knee. Prior to the injury, the instructor had requested the plaintiff to bring a doctor's note explaining what she could and could not do. The plaintiff never complied with this request.

The Court of Appeals upheld the trial court judgment for the defendant stating that both the instructor and the school district were immune from liability for ordinary negligence and that their actions did not constitute willful and wanton misconduct as required by Illinois statute in order to waive immunity and assign liability.

Note. Physical educators and coaches need to adhere to a general rule of requiring any student who is removed from activity by doctor's note to be reinstated only by doctor's note. This is the same for those students who have their activity modified. Always make sure any doctor's excuse has a re-entry date noted on the excuse as was done in this case.

Summers v. Milwaukie Union High School District No. 5
481 P. 2d 369

> Issue: Improper supervision — Failure to furnish doctor
> with list of exercises performed in class

Level of Court: State Court of Appeals
Date/State: 1971/Oregon
Decision: Plaintiff/Affirmed

The plaintiff was injured while performing a springboard exercise in her physical education class. The evidence showed that, as a freshman, the plaintiff was excused from all physical education for the last half of the year by a doctor's note because of a back condition. During her sophomore year, pursuant to a doctor's note, she was excused from doing sit-ups due to a back disability. These doctor's excuses were part of the permanent records on the plaintiff maintained by the district.

The plaintiff complained of back pain during November and December of her junior year and her mother asked the doctor for advice. The doctor requested a list of the exercises the plaintiff was required to perform during physical education. The mother relayed this request to the counselor at school on at least four separate occasions.

On the day of the accident, the plaintiff was required to do a springboard exercise which required her to jump from the springboard, touch her toes in the air and land on her feet. While performing the exercise, the plaintiff lost her balance upon landing, fell backwards and suffered a compression fracture of two vertebrae. The plaintiff's doctor testified that she should not have been doing the springboard exercise and that he would have recommended that she not participate in that exercise had he known she was doing so.

There was no dispute that the girl was required to perform the exercise or that the girl had a previous infirm back condition. The district argued that there was no evidence indicating they knew that the previous back condition created a hazard of injury to the plaintiff. In upholding the trial court judgment for the plaintiff, the Court of Appeals held that, had it not been for the district's failure to furnish the requested list of exercises, the district would have been advised of the hazard by the doctor. The court ruled that "a person is bound not only by what he knows but also by what he might have known through the exercise of ordinary diligence." The court held that the injury to the plaintiff resulting from the springboard exercise was, under all the circumstances, reasonably foreseeable.

Note. This case sounds an obvious warning about communication. While in this case the school district failed to communicate the parent request to the physical educator, teachers and coaches need to take reasonable steps to become informed about the health status of students and athletes in their charge. It could be a mistake for a teacher or a coach to wait for a school nurse or health clerk to notify them of conditions which are noted in the student's health file.

Teachers and coaches need to take the initiative by submitting class and team lists to the school health personnel so that the health records of those students can be quickly reviewed for conditions which have implications for their participation. In some cases, physical educators and coaches may have to accept the responsibility for going through student health folders themselves. Physical educators can also develop medical history and information forms which allow parents to note any medical information or limitations which might have any bearing on their child's participation in the physical education program. These forms should be kept on file in the physical education office. In the event of some limitation being noted on a student health record, and where an injury occurs as a result of that student's or athlete's participation in a restricted activity, the court may be somewhat unsympathetic to a district argument that they were unaware of any limitation.

Toller v. Plainfield School District 202
582 N.E. 2d 237

Issue: Failure to properly match competitors in wrestling

Level of Court: Appellate Court, 3rd District
Date/State: 1991/Illinois
Decision: Defendant/Affirmed

The plaintiff, an 83-pound sixth grader, was injured while wrestling a 100-pound classmate during their physical education class. Testimony at the trial court indicated that the physical education teacher had instructed the class in the basic fundamentals of wrestling following a weekly lesson plan, had demonstrated some of the wrestling maneuvers, had instructed the class not to use illegal moves such as a body slam, and had divided the class into three groups according to an estimation of "size, height, weight, body structure, and ability." At the time of the accident, the instructor was supervising from the edge of the mat approximately 10 feet away.

During the course of the match, the plaintiff received an arm and shoulder injury when his opponent placed his left foot behind the plaintiff's right foot and pushed him backwards. The plaintiff landed on his left arm and his opponent landed across his chest and left shoulder. After hearing the plaintiff screaming in pain, the instructor immediately applied ice and summoned office help.

The plaintiff alleged that the instructor was well aware of the weight classifications used in wrestling and that he chose to disregard them and that by doing so, he improperly and negligently matched the plaintiff and a classmate for competition. Illinois statute provides governmental immunity to school districts and their employees except in cases of willful and wanton misconduct. The trial court granted summary judgment for the defendant.

On appeal, the Appellate Court upheld the summary judgment. The court took note of the fact that the instructor had adequately planned for and instructed the class on fundamentals, had provided warnings against illegal moves, had provided some demonstration of skills, had made an effort to divide the class by both size and ability, had provided supervision, and had administered first aid when required. The court clearly found the teacher's behavior not to be willful and wanton conduct which requires a conscious disregard for the safety and well-being of students.

Note. Had this case taken place in a jurisdiction not covered by governmental immunity, the question of ordinary negligence would have been one for the jury. While it is clear in this case that the teacher knowingly deviated from weight classifications used in the extracurricular program, it is also clear that he did a whole lot right. The importance of written daily lesson plans, as well as unit plans, skill instructions accompanied by demonstrations, safety warnings, attention to size and individual skill differences, and active supervision cannot be overemphasized. Despite not strictly adhering to established weight classifications for competitive wrestling, the instructor in this class established substantial credibility as a reasonable and prudent physical educator.

Benitez v. New York City Board of Education
and the City of New York
543 N.Y.S. 2d 29

Issue: Playing in mismatched game in fatigued condition

Level of Court: Court of Appeals of New York
Date/State: 1988/New York
Decision: Plaintiff/Affirmed/Reversed and dismissed

The plaintiff, a 19-year-old high school football player, received serious injuries as a result of blocking an opposing lineman on a kickoff. Testimony at the trial court indicated that after the 1982 season, the principal of the plaintiff's school had requested the league to drop the school team to a lower division, citing the school's poor record and its string of injuries. The league denied the request and the principal appealed.

On appeal the principal argued that the school's continuance in the same division was unsafe. The appeal was denied and the principal went to the Chancellor's representative with yet another appeal. Again, the injury factor was cited and the principal stated that unless the team was placed in the B Division, the school might suffer an "additional string of serious injuries to our players." A follow-up letter by the principal argued that the team was being asked to continue in the A Division another year and suffer inevitable injuries against much stronger teams. The principal's appeal was again denied. After the decision was made to play the 1983 schedule, the coach stated to the new principal that the upcoming game with JFK High School should not be played and that there was a very high risk of injury. The game was played and the plaintiff received his serious injuries in a accident one minute before the end of the half.

Evidence presented at trial indicated the plaintiff played both offense and defense and was involved in all but 9 of the 56 plays prior to the injury. The coach testified the plaintiff played virtually the whole game because he had no replacement for him other than a 110-pound boy who was physically incapable of playing at that level of competition. Expert testimony claimed that a mismatch, or playing while tired, increased the risk for injury. Expert medical witnesses for the defense conceded that playing while tired would affect the coordination level of a player. The defendants claimed that the plaintiff was a highly-skilled athlete who voluntarily participated, did not complain of being tired and therefore, assumed the risk of injury inherent to the game of football.

The Supreme Court, Appellate Division, upheld the 1.25 million dollar judgment in favor of the plaintiff. In so ruling, the court held that the defendants "unreasonably increased the risk of the plaintiff being injured by playing him in a game between mismatched teams and by playing him virtually the entire game while he was tired." The court, while recognizing that the plaintiff was a voluntary participant, noted that a degree of indirect compulsion existed because of the plaintiff's fear of the negative impact that any refusal to play would have on his standing on the team as well as the impact on the numerous colleges which were actively recruiting him. The plaintiff was held to be 30 percent negligent while the school board was held to 70 percent. The award of damages was adjusted accordingly.

The Court of Appeals of New York reversed the lower court decision and dismissed the complaint. The court held that:

1. The lower court erroneously instructed the jury that a school owes a student voluntarily competing in interscholastic sports the more protective duty and standard of care of a reasonable parent. The Court of Appeals stated that in the context of voluntary participation in sports, the required standard is the less demanding ordinary reasonable care standard against unassumed risks.

2. Voluntary participants in interscholastic athletics assume the risks inherent to the activity provided they are not concealed or unreasonably increased. Fatigue and injuries are both inherent risks to the game of football and therefore, the plaintiff failed to show a causal relation between a negligent act and the injury.

3. The plaintiff failed to show any existence of compulsion. He testified he was "participating voluntarily, that he did not inform his coach of his fatigue, and that he was playing without complaint under the same conditions he had for the previous one and one-half seasons."

The court ruled that the injury was a "luckless accident arising from the vigorous voluntary participation in competitive interscholastic athletics."

Brooks v. Board of Education of the City of New York
189 N.E. 2d 497

Issue: Supervision — Failure to properly match students
for competition

Level of Court: State Court of Appeals
Date/State: 1963/New York
Decision: Plaintiff/Affirmed/Affirmed

The plaintiff was injured in a lead-up game to soccer, known as line soccer. The class was divided into two teams with one on one side of the gymnasium and the other on the opposite side. The boys on each side were randomly given a number. When their number was called, the students would run to the center and attempt to kick the ball through the other team's line. When the plaintiff's number was called he encountered the boy from the other side whose number corresponded with his. The other boy was much taller and heavier than the plaintiff. As a result of this encounter, the plaintiff was kicked in the head and suffered a cerebral concussion and was hospitalized for four days.

The trial court awarded $2,500 in damages for the plaintiff while ruling the defendant negligent in supervising the game as a result of making no attempt to match the boys according to height and weight. The defendant appealed, claiming the plaintiff assumed the risk. The Supreme Court, Appellate Division, ruled the defendant did not request such a ruling at the trial court and was not entitled to do so here. The Supreme Court affirmed the trial court's finding of a prima facie case of negligence. The New York Court of Appeals affirmed the decision of both the lower courts.

Note. The importance of giving some rational thought to the process of matching students for competition or play, where physical contact can become a factor, cannot be over emphasized. While counting off and other random assignment to groups are fast and efficient, they are inappropriate in those situations where height, weight, strength and experience differences can create an increased risk of injury to the participants.

Harrison v. Montgomery County Board of Education
456 A. 2d 894

> Issue: Inadequate supervision — Excessive number of students in gym due to inclement weather

Level of Court: State Court of Appeals
Date/State: 1983/Maryland
Decision: Defendant/Affirmed

The plaintiff, a 14-year-old eighth grade student, received injuries resulting in quadraplegia as a result of participating in activities in his physical education class. The trial court record indicated that due to inclement weather, three physical education teachers brought their classes to the gym to participate in a "free exercise day." A total of 63 students occupied the gymnasium.

As a part of the free exercise day, the teachers allowed students to use any of several pieces of athletic equipment in the gym. The plaintiff, along with several other students, practiced tumbling moves on a 6-8 inch thick crash pad. On the last of several attempts to complete a running front flip, the plaintiff lost control, resulting in the permanent injury.

The plaintiff's suit against the school district and all three of the physical education teachers alleged negligence in allowing the plaintiff to engage in a dangerous activity without proper supervision, in failing to properly train the boy before permitting him to engage in the dangerous activity, in failing to provide proper equipment to prevent injury to the plaintiff and in failing to properly train the defendant teachers.

During the course of the trial, the defendants relied on the doctrine of contributory negligence as a complete defense to the plaintiff's claim. The plaintiff sought to have the jury instructed on the doctrine of comparative negligence, contending the notion of contributory negligence was outmoded and overly harsh. The trial court refused the plaintiff's request for a jury instruction on comparative negligence and returned a verdict in favor of all the defendants.

The plaintiff appealed to the Court of Appeals which upheld the lower court decision. The Court of Appeals ruled that the doctrine of contributory negligence would not be judicially abrogated. The decision to abandon contributory negligence in favor of comparative negligence was held by the court to involve fundamental public policy considerations which should be properly addressed by the state legislature.

Note. The outcome of this case might have been quite different in a jurisdiction not governed by the doctrine of contributory negligence. Those jurisdictions which have retained the concept of contributory negligence deny recovery to a plaintiff who contributed in any measurable way to their own injury.

In a jurisdiction embracing the concept of comparative fault, the jury would have considered the negligence of the defendants in allowing advanced gymnastics stunts to be executed in a crowded facility, with no spotting or active adult supervision, by students who had received little or no instruction or skill lead-up to such advanced stunts as the forward sommersault.

Open gyms are a supervisory nightmare and any activities selected for such settings should be chosen very carefully. Activities of elevated risk are certainly the least desirable in the open gymnasium setting.

Kersey v. Harbin
591 S.W. 2d 745

Issue: Inadequate supervision — Teacher asked to cover two classes at same time

Level of Court: Court of Appeals
Date/State: 1979/Missouri
Decision: Defendant/Reversed and remanded

The plaintiff's son, an eighth grader, became involved in a scuffle during passage from the locker room to the gym. Another student, Steve, stepped on the heels of Daniel's shoes as they headed to the gym. Daniel retaliated by elbowing Steve in the genitals which prompted Steve to pick Daniel up. Daniel subsequently fell or was dropped to the floor. Daniel requested and was given permission to see the nurse. Finding no apparent sign of extreme injury, the nurse permitted Daniel to return to class. When he started to feel worse, Daniel returned to the nurse's office and his parents were summoned. He was taken to his physician and died shortly after from a massive cerebral hemorrhage resulting from a skull fracture. The plaintiffs brought suit against the school superintendent, principal, physical education teachers and the nurse.

The evidence showed that Daniel's regular teacher was absent the day of the accident due to a workshop. The principal had arranged for the other physical education teacher, who shared the same facility, to cover both classes, which was agreeable to both teachers involved. There were between 20-25 students in each of the two classes. The physical education teacher left in charge departed from his normal routine on the day of the accident. His normal practice was to stay in the locker room until everybody was dressed in order to prevent horseplay. On the day of the accident, the teacher instructed his class to proceed to the gym after getting dressed but told Daniel's class to remain in the locker room until everyone was dressed. He then proceeded to join his class in the gym. During the time Daniel's class was unsupervised, the scuffle and resulting injury occurred. Evidence indicated that Steve had been in trouble before.

The defendants filed and received a summary judgment from the trial court. The summary judgment was granted on a number of technical grounds as well as the defendants' claims to governmental immunity. The Appellate Court noted that the rules governing summary judgment against a plaintiff in a tort action state that, "In no case shall a summary judgment be rendered on issues trialable by jury . . . unless the prevailing party is shown by unassailable proof to be entitled thereto as a matter of law." The Court of Appeals rejected the defendants' claim to immunity and held that the defendants owed a supervisory duty of ordinary care. The Court of Appeals reversed the trial judgment and remanded the case for trial with at least two questions to be answered by the jury:

1. Did the superintendent, principal or teachers have actual or constructive knowledge of the quarrelsome and disruptive nature of the student causing the injuries?

2. Given such knowledge, did the defendants take
    appropriate measures to prevent such injuries by
    exercising ordinary care and by supervising
    students?

Note. Although not provided with the analysis and answers to those
questions in this case, the factual situation arising in this case should
certainly alert school administrators, physical educators, and nurses
to a number of policy considerations regarding locker room supervision, the covering of classes for teachers who are absent and the
treatment of head injuries.

Best v. Houtz
541 So. 2d 8

Issue: Supervision — Water on gym floor

Level of Court: State Supreme Court
Date/State: 1989/Alabama
Decision: Defendant/Affirmed

The plaintiff, an eighth grade student, slipped in a puddle of water
during his physical education class and broke his elbow. At the time
of the accident he was playing basketball in the gym and was being
supervised by two physical education instructors. The plaintiff filed
suit against both physical education teachers and the school district
alleging that negligent supervision caused his injuries. The action
against the school district was dismissed because of the district's
statutory immunity against tort claims. The two physical education
teachers moved for summary judgment which was granted by the
trial judge.

The Supreme Court upheld the lower court decision for the two
physical education teaches. The court reviewed trial evidence that
indicated the plaintiff's class was brought indoors because of heavy
rain; one teacher supervised ten boys including the plaintiff who
were playing basketball while the other teacher supervised the other
boys who were waiting for their turn to play; the puddle of water was
located under a ceiling vent; neither the teachers nor the plaintiff saw
the water prior to the accident or saw water dripping from the vent;

both teachers were new to the school and had no knowledge of any problem relative to leaking vents; and both teachers made it their practice to immediately wipe up any water or sweat on the floor if they saw it. In affirming the lower court decision, the Supreme Court stated that all the evidence indicated that neither teacher knew of any water on the floor or of any tendencies for the vents to leak and held that the evidence "showed nothing more than two physical education teachers exercising reasonable and proper supervision" over the class.

Cousins v. Dennis
767 S.W. 2d 296

Issue: Rock thrown by mower

Level of Court: State Supreme Court
Date/State: 1989/Arkansas
Decision: Defendant/Affirmed

The plaintiff was injured as a result of being struck in the left eye by a rock which was thrown by a mower operated by a school district employee. The injury left the plaintiff blind in that eye. Suit was brought against the operator of the mower, the grounds maintenance supervisor, and the school district. The trial court granted the district's motion for summary judgment on the grounds of governmental immunity and also ruled the district was not required to carry liability insurance on the tractor and mower involved in the accident.

The Supreme Court upheld the lower court decision. It held that the Arkansas governmental immunity statute extended immunity to employees engaged in the performance of their duties as well as to the school district itself. The court took note of the plaintiff's claim that all political subdivisions are required to carry motor vehicles liability insurance and that under Arkansas statute, a failure to do so results in the district becoming self-insured and if found negligent, liable up to an amount not to exceed the minimum amounts prescribed in the Motor Vehicle Safety Responsibility Act. The court also noted, however, that implements of husbandry are not required by statute to be registered and, therefore, insured. The court held that the tractor and mower were clearly within the definition of an implement of husbandry and, therefore, were not required to be registered or to carry liability insurance.

Note. While no liability was assigned to the district in this case, the case nonethless provides a valuable reminder to both teachers and coaches. Grounds maintenance staff usually arrive unannounced on school grounds as their schedule is dependent upon weather as well as other variables. It is virtually impossible for teaching and coaching staffs to plan activities around their arrival. Staff would be prudent to stop activities and to have students stand a safe distance away while the immediate playing area is mowed. Do not resume activity until the mower has moved a safe distance away as injuries due to objects being thrown by mowers are foreseeable.

Hanley v. Hornbeck
512 N.Y.S. 2d 262

Issue: Supervision — Fight in class

Level of Court: Supreme Court, Appellate Division
Date/State: 1987/New York
Decision: Defendant/Affirmed

An eighth grade student received injuries to his nose and teeth as a result of being struck in the face by another student during an altercation in their physical education class. The plaintiff charged the district with negligent supervision. Testimony at the trial court indicated the two boys were engaged in a game of whiffleball during their physical education class. An argument over who was going to play catcher arose and some physical contact took place between the boys. As the teacher started to separate the two boys, the plaintiff was struck in the face by the other student.

Evidence indicated that the other boy had previously been involved in a fight (four years earlier) and was referred to the district committee on the handicapped during the sixth grade because of some behavioral traits he exhibited. The district moved for dismissal at the end of the trial. The court reserved a decision on dismissal and allowed the case to go to jury. The jury returned an $8,500 judgment for the plaintiff. The trial court set aside the jury verdict holding that the proximate cause of the plaintiff's injuries was the unforeseen intervention of the other student.

The Appellate Court upheld the lower court decision while finding that the other student's disciplinary record did not show such a strong tendency to engage in violent behavior to warrant his isolation from the regular classroom and that the record indicated that the school committee on the handicapped had, in fact, determined that he should remain schooled with the regular students. The court held that no facts were presented which should have forewarned the district of the risk of assault. The court also noted that the instructor was only 25 feet from the boys when the dispute arose and that he responded immediately. The court found that before the fight had broken out, nothing took place in class which would have signaled the need for closer supervision.

Waechter v. School District No.14-030
733 F. Supp. 1005

Issue: Exercise as punishment

Level of Court: U.S. District Court
Date/State: 1991/Michigan
Decision: Plaintiff

The plaintiff's son, a 13-year-old fifth grade special education student, was ordered by his fifth grade teacher to run what was referred to as the "gut run" as punishment for talking in line at recess. The gut run was a 350 yard sprint which the teacher commonly used for discipline purposes. Students assigned the gut run were required to complete it in less than two minutes.

Evidence indicated that the plaintiff's son was born with a congenital heart defect and had also contracted meningitis which left him with both mental and physical disabilities including legs of unequal length. He was required to wear one leg brace to stabilize ankle movement and was under doctors orders not to participate in competitive contact sports or forced exertion. The student's medical history, including limitations on activity were made known to the defendants. As a result of his required participation in the gut run, the plaintiff's son suffered cardiac arrhythmia and died.

The plaintiffs brought action in Federal Court against the school district, board of education, superintendent, principal and teacher. In their complaint the plaintiffs alleged that the defendants violated their son's constitutional right to substantive due process and procedural due process under the 14th Amendment as well as his rights under the Federal Rehabilitation Act of 1973 as it relates to discrimination on the basis of handicap. They also alleged wrongful death under the Michigan wrongful death statute.

The school district filed a motion to have the case dismissed. The U.S. District Court ruled that the complaint stated a proper claim for violation of substantive due process under the 14th Amendment of the U.S. Constitution which provides that no state can deprive any individual of life, liberty, or property without due process of law. The court dismissed the allegations related to procedural due process while noting Michigan law allows civil procedure to address alleged excessive or unjustified punishment. The federal court dismissed the charges alleging violation of the Rehabilitation Act and declined to accept jurisdiction over the wrongful death claim because it involved questions of law unique to Michigan regarding immunity and other defenses to immunity.

Note. In another punishment case, Jackson v. Wooster Board of Education, 504 N.E. 2d 1144 (Ohio, 1985) a student was ordered to do 25 push-ups, nude, on the locker room floor as punishment for taking two towels after showering instead of one. He was ridiculed by the teacher as he performed the punishment in full view of the class. In this case the student sued charging intentional infliction of emotional harm.

The use of exercise as punishment by those in the physical education and sport profession, as well as by those outside the profession, continues as a problem. Exercise as punishment is an outdated and risky strategy. It is pedagogically weak and counterproductive to the goals of physical education and sport programs which strive to teach students and athletes that exercise is a healthy and enjoyable activity and a means to a desired goal of personal fitness and wellness. Prescriptions of exercise for the purpose of punishment increase the susceptibility of physical educators and coaches to lawsuits because such prescriptions are often quite large, often carried out with little or no supervision, and have the potential to make the student the object of ridicule.

As states continue to revise statutes relative to corporal punishment, exercise as punishment has received some attention. Both California and Oregon have enacted legislation prohibiting corporal punishment and have included exercise as punishment within the definition of corporal punishment thereby making its use illegal.

Metzger v. Osbeck
841 F. 2d 518

Issue: Excessive force in corporal punishment

Level of Court: U.S. Court of Appeals, Third Circuit
Date/State: 1988/Pennsylvania
Decision: Defendant/Reversed and remanded in part and affirmed in part

The plaintiff filed a civil rights action under the 5th and 14th Amendments as a result of injuries received when disciplined by his physical education teacher. Evidence submitted at trial alleged that the plaintiff was failing his swimming class because of his failure to participate. On the day of the accident, the last day of the grading period, the class was engaged in a recreational swim. The plaintiff had a note excusing him from class due to illness and a swollen leg. He was on the pool deck during class trading baseball cards with several other members of the class. The teacher was talking to a student several feet away when he heard the plaintiff using inappropriate language in his conversation with a female student. The teacher walked up behind the plaintiff and placed his arms around the neck and shoulder area and asked the boy if he was the one using foul language. While reprimanding him for the inappropriate language, the teacher's arm moved upward from the boy's Adam's apple to under his chin, causing the plaintiff to stand on his toes. When the teacher released the plaintiff he fell face down onto the pool deck having lost consciousness at some point. As a result of the incident, the plaintiff suffered a broken nose, fractured teeth and other injuries that required hospitalization.

The trial court granted summary judgment to all defendants. It ruled that there were no due process violations and that the evidence would not allow a jury to infer that the teacher intended to injure the student or that he acted in reckless disregard of a risk of which he should have been aware. The summary judgment for the district and board of education was granted because there was no school policy that authorized the teacher's conduct and, therefore, no legal or factual basis for vicarious liability.

The U.S. Court of Appeals upheld the summary judgment for the district and school board but reversed the judgment for the teacher and remanded that portion of the case for further proceedings. The court ruled that "a decision to discipline a student, if accomplished through excessive force and appreciable physical pain, may constitute an invasion of the child's 5th Amendment liberty interest in his personal security and a violation of substantive due process prohibited by the 14th Amendment."

The court held that even if physical discipline is pedagogically appropriate and condoned by district policy, a jury could find the force used by the teacher exceeded that which was needed. The court held that if it could be shown a teacher intended to cause harm, the teacher "would be subject to liability for crossing the constitutional line separating a common law tort from a deprivation of substantive due process." The court concluded that the summary judgment granted by the lower court could not be permitted to stand where "a defendant who by an intentional act may have caused serious harm, just because [the defendant] claims he did not intend the harm."

Note: Physical contact in disciplining students should only occur when it is necessary for the physical safety of other students or the teacher. Even in those cases, the physical force applied should only be that which is reasonably required to maintain safety and order. Physical force applied against students in any other circumstance is likely to leave the teacher's or coach's actions open to close scrutiny by the courts.

Bauer v. Minidoka School District No. 331
778 P. 2d 336

Issue: Negligent supervision — Football game before the start of school

Level of Court: State Supreme Court
Date/State: 1989/Idaho
Decision: Defendant/Reversed and remanded

The plaintiff, a junior high student, suffered a broken leg as a result of falling over a sprinkler pipe while engaged in an informal game of football on the school grounds before the start of classes. Suit was filed against the school district alleging inadequate supervision, improper storing of sprinkler pipes, failing to properly maintain grounds in a safe condition and failing to warn of the dangers posed by the pipes on the playing field. The district moved for summary judgment claiming it owed no duty to the plaintiff because of the state recreational user statute which limits the liability of landowners for injuries on land used for recreational purposes.

The district argued that the football game fell under the recreational user statute because it occurred before official school hours, was not organized by school officials and the participants provided their own equipment as well as supervision and control of the game. The plaintiff argued against the motion for summary judgment charging that the game was regularly played between 8-8:30 and included students who arrived by school bus by 8:00 a.m., that the principal and several teachers who arrived early in the morning knew the game was being played and watched the game on several occasions and that the principal had made it clear to students and staff that the game was only to be played on the football field and nowhere else. The motion for summary judgment was granted on the basis of the recreational user statute.

On appeal, the Supreme Court held that the recreational user statute did not apply. The court ruled that "when the principal is present, some faculty are on duty and students have arrived, the school day has begun and the recreational user statute has no application." The court held that the complaint adequately pleaded a claim for negligent supervision. The court reversed the summary judgment and remanded it to the trial court for further proceedings stating "if the district had a duty to supervise the students in the football game, and if the district should have reasonably foreseen the dangers that existed when the game was played on the field where the sprinkler pipes were stored, but failed to take precautions to protect the participants, the district breached its duty to supervise the students there."

Laneheart v. Orleans Parish School Board
524 So. 2d 138

Issue: Supervision of playground before school

Level of Court: Circuit Court of Appeals
Date/State: 1988/Louisiana
Decision: Defendant/Reversed

The plaintiff, a 10-year-old elementary school student, cut his face as a result of a fall on the school playground. He arrived for the breakfast program at 8:00 a.m. and after finishing breakfast, he went outside to play. While playing football, he got into a scuffle with another student, fell and cut his face on some glass and rocks. At the time of the accident, no teacher was on duty on the playground. The parents brought suit claiming inadequate supervision as well as allowing a hazardous condition (pile of broken glass and rocks) to exist on the playground. The trial court ruled that the district is not an insurer of student safety and that the injury was the result of the plaintiff fighting. The trial judge dismissed the case and the parents appealed.

The Court of Appeals ruled that while the plaintiff failed to prove that school authorities had actual or constructive knowledge of the hazardous condition on the playground, its presence was irrelevant because the school board was liable for failing to maintain adequate supervision of the students. In so holding, the court stated that "while there is generally no duty to supervise the school grounds after school hours. . . it must provide supervision for children who are waiting on the grounds for the school bus or participating in an after-hours activity sanctioned by the school." While testimony indicated that children were not allowed to go outside after breakfast until the 8:30 bell rang, the evidence clearly indicated that there were a number of children on the playground at 8:20 when the accident occurred and that no staff member was present. The Appellate Court rendered judgment for the plaintiff while holding that parents should be able to expect that their children will be supervised from the time the breakfast program begins until the students leave the grounds to go home and that adequate supervision would have prevented the plaintiff's injury.

Augustus v. Joseph A. Craig Elementary School
459 So. 2d 665

Issue: Supervision of after-school practice for elementary school students

Level of Court: Court of Appeals
Date/State: 1984/Louisiana
Decision: Plaintiff/Affirmed

The Court of Appeals upheld a trial court decision holding a public school liable for negligent supervision when a six-year-old student was injured while attending a track practice run by an independent group not formally connected to the school. The boy returned to the school grounds 30 minutes after school was out. While waiting for the coaches to arrive, a number of the children began to play with a tether ball pole that was a four-foot section of rod iron imbedded in a tire filled with concrete.

While rolling the pole and standard on its side, several of the students, including the plaintiff, jumped over it. As he was jumping, the plaintiff fell and the tire rolled on his head. Evidence presented at trial indicated that the independent group, the Tambourine and Fan Club, worked with the principal and teachers of the school to sponsor athletic events and educational programs. This was done with the approval of the district superintendent. The track practice was announced by the principal over the public address system to students. The teachers distributed flyuers that both advertised the practice and solicited parent permission. The flyer advised parents that while this was a club activity staffed by the club and not the school, there would be tight supervision.

The court ruled that while ordinarily there is no duty to supervise the grounds after school hours, the involvement of school staff in promoting the track practice and their written assurance that there would be tight supervision made them liable for any breach of the duty to supervise.

Pomrehn v. Crete-Monee High School District
427 N.E. 2d 1387

Issue: Lack of supervision before practice

Level of Court: District Court of Appeals
Date/State: 1981/Illinois
Decision: Defendant/Affirmed

A member of the high school girls' softball team received serious head injuries when she fell off the trunk of a moving car while awaiting the arrival of the coach for practice. Trial court evidence indicated that the coach worked in a split-shift attendance situation and that teachers in this situation were required to stay at school until 5:45, although it was common for them to leave at 5:30 when classes ended for students. The softball team practiced at an elementary school which was less than a mile from the high school.

Prior to the day of the accident, the coach had left school at 5:30 and arrived at the practice field by 5:35. Practice was scheduled to start at 5:50. The day before the accident, the school principal informed the coach that she was to remain at school until the required 5:45 time. The coach claims this action was taken for harassment purposes in retaliation for several discrimination suits filed by the coach against the district. When asked by the coach what happens if one of the students gets hurt, the principal replied they won't.

On the day of the accident, the coach arrived at 5:45 just after the plaintiff fell from the top of the trunk of the car on which she was riding. The plaintiff alleged that the district was negligent and guilty of willful and wanton misconduct for requiring the coach to stay at school until 5:45 when it knew or should have known that this action increased the risk of injury to the softball players.

The Appellate Court upheld the lower court summary judgment for the defendant school district. The court held that in order to state a claim for willful and wanton misconduct, the plaintiff must show an intentional act or one which indicates a reckless or conscious disregard of probable injury. The court ruled there was no evidence of special dangers, prior problems with the softball team members or hazards with the practice area and that the district's behavior had, therefore, not shown reckless or conscious disregard of probable dangers.

Note. Supervision needs to be provided for a reasonable amount of time both before and after practice sessions. It is prudent to provide supervision from the time school is dismissed up to the start of an after school practice, through the practice session, and up to the point when the last student has left the facility after the practice session is over. Whenever a time lag exists between the end of the school day and the start of practice (such as evening practice), clear expectations about arrival time should be communicated to all athletes. The coach should arrive 10-15 minutes before team members are scheduled to arrive.

Banks v. Terrebonne Parish School Board
339 So. 2d 1295

Issue: Supervision — Before the formal start of class

Level of Court: Court of Appeals
Date/State: 1976/Louisiana
Decision: Defendant/Affirmed

The plaintiff was injured while attempting a dive forward roll over three folding chairs which were stacked on top of one another. The plaintiff approached the stacked chairs and bounced off a springboard. His feet struck the stack of chairs which caused him to land on his head. He suffered a slight subluxation of the cervical spine and after a 10-day hospital stay, he fully recovered. At the time of the accident, the teacher was on the stage at the other end of the gym collecting valuables from students who were dressing down. He did not see the accident but after being informed, he immediately sent the boy to the office and the parents were notified.

Evidence at trial indicated that the plaintiff was in violation of class rules which authorized students to participate in tumbling only after they had dressed down, roll had been taken and the teacher was available for supervision. The plaintiff had violated all three parts of this rule. The evidence established that the teacher was well qualified and that the class was properly instructed. The trial court dismissed the case while finding no negligence on the part of the teacher or the school district.

The Court of Appeals upheld the trial court decision holding that the law does not require that each student be personally supervised every moment. It ruled that the teacher had properly instructed the class in tumbling and had established clear rules regarding participation in class and that the teacher was unaware of the plaintiff's activity because he was engaged in reasonable tasks in preparation for the start of class.

Note. While no liability was assessed in this case, physical educators would be well advised to plan for the maximum supervision of students. Collecting of valuables on the stage not only left the gym area unsupervised but the locker room as well. Teachers would be well advised not only to develop clear classroom expectations as was done in this case, but to make every attempt to put themselves in a position to observe whether or not the expectations are being adhered to. Having some students in the locker room, some in the gym, and some at the stage makes the duty of supervision a difficult one at best.

Campbell v. Montgomery City Board of Education
533 A. 2d 9

> Issue: Lack of supervision — Girl sexually assaulted in boys locker room

Level of Court: Court of Special Appeals
Date/State: 1987/Maryland
Decision: Defendant/Vacated in part, reversed and
               remanded in part

The plaintiff, a 13-year-old girl, was sexually assaulted after entering a boys locker room during her physical education class period. Trial court evidence established that the plaintiff was excused from participating in class due to a broken finger. She was in the gym when class began but left the class and went outside to the playing field, where the boys physical education teacher ordered her to go back to her class. She returned to the building and entered the boys locker room, something she admitted to having done on four other occasions. After entering the locker room on the day of the incident, the plaintiff heard someone coming. She went into an old shower area, which was off limits to students, and squeezed her way into a small space between the lockers and the edge of the wall. She was followed by a male student, and the plaintiff and the male student were kissing when another male student entered the area. The second student pulled the girl onto his lap and began molesting her. As the plaintiff screamed, a group of about 15 students entered the area and a number of them also began to molest her. Evidence indicated the plaintiff screamed several times while the boys attempted to cover her mouth. During the assault, the boys teacher was still on the playing field.

When the teacher finally entered the locker room he heard some noise coming from the restricted area and yelled for whoever was back there to get out. He saw four or five students squeeze out of the area, then listened for a few seconds, and warned that there better not be anyone else in there. He did not question those who exited about what they were doing. When the bell rang, the teacher watched the boys exit and then went to the office on an errand. On his way back to the locker room he was told by a student there was a girl in the boys locker room. By the time he got there, the plaintiff had left and gone back to the gym, where a substitute noticed her appearance and asked what had happened. The plaintiff said she had hurt her foot and the substitute, not satisfied with her story, took her to the office. The plaintiff was suspended for five days for entering the boys locker room.

The plaintiff brought suit charging negligence on the part of the teacher and school district for inadequate supervision. Suit was also filed against six students. The jury returned a verdict for the plaintiff and awarded the girl and her mother nearly $309,000 in damages. The trial judge set aside the verdict against both the district and the teacher while allowing a $10,000 judgment against one of the students to stand. In doing so, the trial judge held that the girl was both contributorily negligent and assumed the risk of harm when she entered the boys locker room. The judge supported his ruling on the basis that the girl was intelligent, had engaged in voluntary sex previously, and had been raped previously. The judge ruled that based on her experience, she should have foreseen the risk to which she was exposing herself. Contributory negligence and assumption of risk both serve as bars to recovery under Maryland tort law.

The Court of Appeals vacated the lower court decision and re-entered the judment of the plaintiff. The court held that the questions of contributory negligence and assumption of risk are normally questions for the jury and not the court. The Appellate Court stated that because the plaintiff had entered the locker room on previous occasions without incident, it was reasonable to assume that she did not foresee the risk of sexual assault by doing so. The court held that the plaintiff could not be held to be contributorily negligent or said to have assumed the risk as a matter of law and, therefore, the decision was one for the jury. The court ruled that the liability of the school district and the teacher might be limited by the state statute to $100,000. The question of a liability cap and whether it applied to the school board as well as the teacher was remanded back to the trial court for determination.

Note: Locker rooms should either be supervised or kept locked, as they represent one of the more potentially dangerous rooms in a school facility. If left unattended, they easily lend themselves to horseplay.

Several factors contribute to the danger of the locker room area, including the typically smooth, polished-surface concrete floor, which is easy to clean but extremely slick when wet. Locker rooms tend to be somewhat congested when used by classes, and crowding in confined areas tends to foster pushing, shoving, and rough play by students, especially during unstructured time like the dressing period. Within the locker room, several potentially dangerous items can be found, such as the lockers themselves, wire baskets for clothing, laundry carts, towels, benches, trash cans, and sinks, which lend themselves to horseplay.

In addition to the physical dangers provided by locker rooms, they can become a dangerously secluded area when not in use by a physical education class or athletic team. If left open during the day and into the evening hours, as is often the case in secondary schools, access by students as well as nonschool people could become a problem. Physical assaults, sexual assaults, hazing, and drug trafficking are not uncommon occurrences in our schools. It is certainly foreseeable that activities such as these are more likely to occur in the seclusion offered by areas such as restrooms and locker rooms that are left open and unsupervised.

IN SUMMARY

THE REASONABLY PRUDENT PHYSICAL EDUCATOR OR COACH:

1. Develops comprehensive class, team and locker room rules and procedures and effectively communicates those to students and athletes. Establishes clear rules relative to all equipment use.

2. Strictly and consistently enforces all established class, team, and school rules.

3. Provides active supervision required within the scope of his/her employment whether in the gym, on the field, in the locker room, or in the hall. The teacher is where he/she is assigned and on time. Provides general as well as specific supervision.

4. Does not unnecessarily absent him/herself from classes or practice sessions. Gives consideration to age and composition of the group, past experience with the group, the nature of the activity and the equipment being used, and the reason and duration for any temporary absence before leaving the group for any reason.

Continued

5. Assigns only qualified personnel to conduct and supervise activities.

6. Does not allow students to engage in unreasonably dangerous activities.

7. Is aware of the health status of all students under his/her charge and provides modified activity or exclusion from activity where appropriate.

8. Carefully matches students and athletes in any activity involving potential contact, giving consideration to age, size, skill, and experience differences.

9. Keeps activities within the ability level of individual students.

10. Refrains from all use of physical discipline and punishment, including the use of exercise as punishment.

11. Does not attempt to supervise more than one area at a time.

12. Immediately attends to any dangerous situations.

EQUIPMENT, GROUNDS, FACILITIES

Physical education and sport personnel owe a duty to their students and athletes of conducting their classes, practices, and games in a safe learning and play environment. In providing a safe environment, a number of responsibilities come into existence.

Physical educators and coaches must share in the responsibility to check, on a regular basis, the grounds, facilities, and equipment used in delivering their programs to students. Any dangerous condition found to exist within the grounds or facilities should be reported immediately and measures taken to correct the condition before allowing the participation of students in or on them. The mere reporting of a dangerous condition is not enough to relieve the physical educator or coach of liability in the event of a mishap. It would be a serious mistake to continue to use an area or facility while waiting for corrective measures to be taken. If the condition represents a significant risk to the safety of students, given the activity in which they are engaged, the instructor would be well advised to either alter the activity or make arrangements to use or share another facility. Likewise, worn, broken or defective equipment should be either repaired or replaced immediately. Continued use of such equipment while awaiting repair or replacement would be a serious error and one hard to justify before a court.

A number of activities including football, soccer, baseball/softball, floor hockey, wrestling, volleyball, and gymnastics require some degree of safety equipment in order to assure reasonably safe participation by all students. Age, skill, experience, and level of play will all play a role in determining the level of risk and the type and amount of safety equipment needed. Lack of funds would be a poor argument to use in justifying the failure to supply students and athletes with such equipment.

Physical education and sport staff need to take care in not turning an otherwise safe facility into a dangerous one through the inappropriate arrangement of equipment or use of the facility. The facility should provide adequate space for participation relative to both the number of students and the activity in which the students are engaged. Given the activity, equipment should be arranged in a manner which allows for safe movement and traffic patterns. The equipment should be arranged in a manner which allows for a safe zone between activity boundaries and all walls or other obstacles which may be an obstruction to safe movement. When selecting an activity for any facility or when arranging the equipment for student participation consideration must be afforded to the known phenomenon that students will get pushed, bumped and will trip, fall and over-run boundaries and bases.

While product liability has become a major concern for manufacturers of athletic and physical education equipment, it also has some implications for physical educators and coaches at the building level. As suppliers of equipment to students, school districts and physical education/sport personnel need to take care in not supplying equipment which is dangerous for its intended use. It is going to become increasingly important that those responsible for ordering equipment pay attention to the design of that equipment and the track record and reputation of the companies from whom they order. This is a relatively new area of concern for people at the building level but has the potential for real risk.

An attractive nuisance is an instrumentality (equipment) or a condition on the premises which may be reasonably expected to be a source of danger to trespassing children and which may be reasonably expected to attract them to the premises. There have been a number of cases involving physical education, sport, and playground equipment over the years where plaintiffs have charged school districts with maintaining an attractive nuisance. Even in those jurisdictions where governmental immunity applies, liability will generally be assigned where it is shown that an attractive nuisance existed. The most common charges of attractive nuisance in the physical education and sport settings have identified defective playground equipment and gymnastics apparatus.

In applying the attractive nuisance doctrine to child trespassers, the courts have used a four point test to determine liability. The four conditions necessary for liability under this doctrine are:

1. The place where the condition is found must be one upon which the possessor of the land either knows or has reason to know that children are likely to trespass;
2. The condition must be one which the possessor of the land should recognize as an unreasonable risk of harm to such child trespassers;

3. The child, because of his/her immaturity does not understand or fully appreciate the danger involved; and
4. The necessity of the possessor of the land to maintain the condition must be slight compared to the risk of children which are involved.[16]

The attractive nuisance doctrine will rarely apply in the physical education, sport or playground setting as children almost always enter school grounds and facilities as invitees and therefore fail to meet the trespass requirement for application of the doctrine. Such is the case whenever the child comes onto the school playground or playing field which is generally held to be open to the public whether during or after school hours. A student may become a licensee when entering an area of the premises that he or she is not authorized to enter. Rarely do they become trespassers.

Despite the general lack of applicability of the attractive nuisance doctrine in the physical education and sport setting, physical educators and coaches would be prudent to take note of the above four point test for liability under the attractive nuisance doctrine. Steps should be taken to secure or otherwise make inaccessible any equipment or apparatus within a facility which might be accessed by students and which presents any unreasonable risk of harm to those students who, because of their immaturity, do not recognize or fully appreciate the dangers involved. For example, leaving trampolines unsecured within a gym or apparatus room invites potentially tragic consequences. When not in use, trampolines should be locked in a closed position within a locked facility. Hurdles, high jump and vaulting pits, blocking sleds, and portable steel goals are often left out rather than stored during their seasons of use. Again, physical educators, coaches and their school districts would be prudent to secure such equipment in some manner so as to make it unusable by children visiting the premises.

The following cases have dealt with the various issues relating to equipment, grounds and facilities and offer a number of policy implications for physical educators, coaches and school districts.

Shearer v. Perry Community School District
236 N.W. 2d 688

Issue: Equipment — Universal Gym

Level of Court: State Supreme Court
Date/State: 1975/Iowa
Decision: Defendant/Affirmed

The plaintiff, a 14-year-old high school student, lost his front two teeth when a portion of a Universal Gym became disengaged from the rest of the apparatus and struck him in the mouth. The injury took place on March 25, 1971. On March 28, 1973, the plaintiff filed suit against the school district and both the manufacturer and distributor of the exercise machine for $25,000 in damages. The plaintiff alleged negligence, breach of implied warranty and strict liability.

The district denied liability and later filed a motion for summary judgment claiming the plaintiff had not complied with the notice requirement of the Tort Claims Act. The statutory notice requirement mandated that claims against public bodies be commenced within six months unless notice of claim was served within 60 days. If the notice was properly served, the law required that the action be commenced within two years. The plaintiff filed no such notice but asserted the school district, through its agents and employees, had actual notice of the injury and that the time for bringing the action should be extended to two years pursuant to the above statute. The trial court granted summary judgment for the defendant ruling that actual notice of the injury by the teacher and other agents of the school district and verbal notice to the superintendent did not fulfill the statutory requirements of notice.

The Supreme Court affirmed the lower court decision, ruling that notice of the injury by the district, its agents and employees, did not meet the statutory requirement of presenting written notice of a tort claim. The court also held that the notice statute did not violate the due process and equal protection clauses of the U.S. Constitution as claimed by the defendants.

The Supreme Court overruled its holding on the constitutionality of the above notice requirement eleven years later in the case of Miller v. Boone County Hospital, 394 N.W. 2d 776, 1986. In Boone, the court ruled that the section of the Tort Claims Act requiring actions against public bodies to be commenced within six months or notice of claim to be served within sixty days of injury violated the Equal Protection Clause of both the U.S. and the state of Iowa constitutions. The court noted that the statute of limitations which applies to the private sector would serve to prevent "stale claims" against the state and that to have a more stringent statute of limitations in the public sector denied equal protection and due process under the law.

Note. Teachers and coaches should always instruct their students and athletes to check each piece of apparatus or weight room equipment prior to using it. A quick check to make sure that barbell collars and all handles, bars or removable parts of stationary exercise machines are secure will substantially reduce the risk of accidents such as the one in this case. In addition to instructing students on the "how" and "why" of checking weight room equipment, physical educators and coaches should conduct a daily examination of weight room facilities looking for worn, broken or loose parts on all weight room equipment. Close supervision, adequate instruction, and close attention to the state of the weight room and all equipment within it, are essential to the safe and prudent operation of this type of facility.

Gore v. Bethlehem Area School District
537 A. 2d 913

Issue: Equipment — Portable chinning bar

Level of Court: Commonwealth Court of Pennsylvania
Date/State: 1988/Pennsylvania
Decision: Defendant/Affirmed

The plaintiff, an elementary student, was injured when a removable chin-up bar, located in a doorway between the gym and equipment room, became dislodged and struck the plaintiff in the mouth. The trial court granted summary judgment for the school district, dismissing the action on the grounds of school district immunity. In Pennsylvania, school districts are immune from liability for instruction and supervision. Immunity of school districts is only denied where there is negligence in allowing school property to be unsafe for the activities for which it is regularly used. The court agreed with the district that the "portable chinning bar" did not constitute real property and immunity was, therefore, granted.

Note. No discussion of the safety of equipment, instruction and supervision took place because of the decision on immunity. This case, nonetheless, sounds a warning for physical educators. Portable equipment such as this is very common in schools, especially elementary schools where space is at a premium. In the same manner as gymnastics equipment and exercise machines, equipment such as portable chinning bars need to be checked regularly and students need to be instructed on how to check the equipment themselves to ensure that it is secure and safe for use. Closer supervision of activities often becomes necessary when using any equipment or apparatus which is not a permanent fixture.

Koch v. City of Avon Board of Education
580 N.E. 2d 809

Issue: Failure to repair worn Rheuther board

Level of Court: Court of Appeals
Date/State: 1989/Ohio
Decision: Defendant/Affirmed

The plaintiff, a 15-year-old freshman, injured his knee while performing a squat vault over a horse in his physical education class. Trial evidence indicated that the class in question began with a lecture on the use of the equipment and safety instructions followed by a teacher demonstration of the vaulting exercises and then by student practice. The plaintiff had successfully completed five squat vaults as well as two other vaults, which were advanced variations of the squat vault, prior to the accident. Testimony indicated that the rubber on the bottom of the Rheuther board had become unglued. The teacher testified that he "believed the Rheuther board worked better with a heavy horsehair mat underneath it and that he therefore did not ask to have it repaired or replaced when the rubber on the bottom of the board became unglued."

The trial court granted summary judgment for the defendants based on their claim of governmental immunity. The court based its decision on the statute conferring immunity where injury results from the exercise of judgment or discretion in the determination of how to use equipment. The court found that the school board relied on the instructor's expertise in evaluating whether to repair or replace equipment and in determining how equipment would be used. The Court of Appeals upheld the summary judgment for the defendants issued by the lower court.

Note. Physical educators would be wise to not disregard the need to replace or repair equipment when it shows signs of wear and tear. The cost of repair to the Rheuther board in this case would have been extremely slight, especially compared to the potential loss from injury resulting from ignoring the repair needs. Absent immunity protection, a jury might very well have found a basis for liability in this case.

Cestari v. School District of Cheltenham Township
520 A. 2d 110

Issue: Inadequate equipment — Pole vault pit

Level of Court: Commonwealth Court
Date/State: 1987/Pennsylvania
Decision: Defendant/Reversed and remanded

The plaintiff received injuries while competing in the pole vault for his school team. At the time of the accident, he failed to clear the bar and landed with one foot on and one foot off the landing mat. The plaintiff filed suit charging the district with negligence for failing to conform to applicable guidelines related to the placement of the landing mat and the number of mats used both in and around the pole vault pit. He also charged negligence in failing to properly maintain the pit.

The trial court granted the district's motion for summary judgment based on governmental immunity and dismissed the case. The Appellate Court agreed with the plaintiff that the maintenance of the pole vault pit fell within the real property exception to immunity. The court held that because proper matting constituted an essential safety element of the school grounds being used for vaulting, this case could come within the real property exception to immunity and that the adequacy of mat protection was a material issue of fact to be decided by the jury and not by the court via summary judgment. The case was remanded to the trial court for further proceedings.

Ohnstad v. Omaha Public School District No. 1
442 N.W. 2d 859

Issue: Placement of pole vault standards and proper pole for weight of vaulter

---

Level of Court: State Supreme Court
Date/State: 1989/Nebraska
Decision: Defendant/Affirmed

The plaintiff's son, a pole vaulter on the high school track team, received fatal head injuries while vaulting in his conference track meet. Suit was filed against both the host school district and the boy's school district. The complaint charged that the head track coach failed to properly supervise and instruct the pole vault event. The complaint specifically charged that the defendants were negligent in:

1. Failing to properly staff the event with qualified coaches;
2. Failing to properly instruct and warn of the risks involved in the pole vault;
3. Failing to properly give instructions in the techniques of vaulting;
4. Failing to properly supervise the event;
5. Failing to give instructions in the proper placement of the pole vault standards; and
6. Failing to provide proper and safe equipment.

The trial court dismissed the case against the Omaha School District after its motion for summary judgment was granted and the case was continued against the plaintiff's school district. The evidence at trial only focused on two of the five allegations. The plaintiff contended that the coach placed the standards too far forward and that his son was too heavy for the pole which was supplied to him. The boy was injured when he fell head first into the metal planting box. The trial court found for the defendants and held that injuries were the result of the boy's own "action of jumping with a low, late plant and attempting to complete the vault after he had made the [poor] pole plant." The court ruled that the defendants' negligence, if any, was not the proximate cause of the accident.

The plaintiff appealed contending the evidence was not sufficient to support the finding of the lower court. The Court of Appeals upheld the lower court decision while stating that factual findings of a lower court will only be set aside where they are clearly incorrect. The court held that sufficient evidence was presented to support the trial court conclusions. Specifically, the court took note of three expert witnesses who said the accident was "the result of a low, late pole plant and that the placement of the standards did not contribute to the accident." They also noted the testimony of two experts who testified the boy was using the proper pole at the time of the accident.

Woodson v. North Chicago Community
School District No. 64
543 N.E. 2d 290

> Issue: Inappropriate equipment — Hurdle in
> physical education class

Level of Court: District Appellate Court
Date/State: 1989/Illinois
Decision: Defendant/Affirmed

A 9-year-old boy received injuries in his physical education class when he tripped and fell over a hurdle being used for a relay race in the gymnasium. The plaintiff filed suit charging the district had a duty to provide appropriate equipment including safety padding and protective equipment to prevent student injury. It was alleged that the defendants breached this duty by:

1. Not supplying a padded running surface;
2. Not supplying mats to cushion the hard gymnasium floor;

3. Not providing personal protective equipment such as knee pads.

The trial court dismissed the case while ruling that the district had governmental immunity in cases of ordinary negligence except in those cases where the district supplies defective equipment or fails to provide effective equipment to guard against injuries which are severe and common to the activity being engaged in. The court held the plaintiff did not allege that the injury received was a common one and one which could have been prevented by the equipment specified. The plaintiff filed an amended complaint charging that he received both severe and permanent knee injuries which were a foreseeable, common and severe result of tripping over a hurdle during a race. The district again moved for dismissal of the case arguing it was immune to suit for ordinary negligence and that conducting a hurdle race on a gym floor does not constitute negligence. The court dismissed the complaint again but granted the plaintiff the right to amend the complaint a second time. The plaintiff's second amended complaint elaborated on the nature of the injuries but was also dismissed for failing to allege specific facts that showed the injury was "common, severe and permanent."

The Appellate Court upheld the lower court decision. Illinois law grants immunity to school districts for ordinary negligence. Districts and their employees are liable only for willful and wanton misconduct. Illinois courts have carved out two exceptions to this rule. The courts have required districts to supply athletic equipment which is fit for its intended purpose and to supply necessary safety equipment. The court ruled that the plaintiff's charge that the injury was common and severe and that it was foreseeable was insufficient to state a cause of action. The court suggested a number of facts which needed to be pleaded in order to state a possible cause of action. Among these were:

1. The height of the hurdle;
2. The number of hurdles;
3. Distance between the hurdles;
4. Other activities required in the relay before encountering the hurdle;
5. Whether this was a training session where tripping could be expected; and

6. Whether the plaintiff was physically capable of participating safely.

The court also noted that the plaintiff failed to support with facts that a fractured knee cap is a common injury resulting from hurdling or that padding and mats are commonly used in hurdling.

Montag v. Board of Education, School District No. 40
446 N.E. 2d 299

> Issue: Improper supervision and inadequate safety equipment —
> Still rings during team practice

Level of Court: Court of Appeals
Date/State: 1983/Illinois
Decision: Defendant/Affirmed

The plaintiff, a 16-year-old member of the gymnastics team, suffered paralysis as a result of a fall from the still rings. On the day of the accident, the plaintiff was practicing for the upcoming district competition. Testimony at the trial court indicated that the rings were between 7 and 8 feet above the ground, two one-inch rubber mats and one four-inch landing mat were underneath the rings, and the coach was acting as a spotter. Testimony also showed that the plaintiff was not inexperienced. He had been on the team for three months and had prior experience on the rings in his physical education class which was taught by the coach. The injury occurred during the plaintiff's dismount at the end of his routine. The dismount was of intermediate difficulty and had been mastered two weeks before the injury. The coach was unable to reach the plaintiff before he landed on his back and received his injuries. The plaintiff brought suit against the coach and the board claiming they failed to properly supervise the plaintiff and failed to ensure proper use of the safety equipment in the gym. The board was charged with a failure to supply the gym with adequate safety equipment. The plaintiff further alleged that the conduct of the defendants was willful and wanton.

The Appellate Court upheld the trial court decision for the defendants. The court ruled that the defendants were immune from suit except for willful and wanton misconduct and that the evidence failed to show that the defendants' conduct rose to that level. In looking at the charge against the district for failing to supply the gym with adequate safety equipment, the court noted expert testimony for the plaintiff which indicated the gym as a whole was unsafe due to a lack of adequate mats for each piece of equipment, a lack of a safety belt to be used in learning the various skills employed in routines, and inadequate matting under the rings to prevent injury. The court ruled, however, that the issue at hand was one of causation and that the plaintiff "extended the causational chain too far into the abstract." The court held that the issue was not whether the gym as a whole was unsafe but whether there was adequate matting under the rings. The court accepted the defendants' evidence that the amount of matting used was the same as employed in competition and was adequate. Regarding the use of a safety belt, the court noted that a safety belt would not have normally been used at the time of the routine and dismount and that it could only speculate what prior use of a safety belt could have done for the plaintiff.

Parisi v. Harpursville Central School District
553 N.Y.S. 2d 566

Issue: Failure to provide catcher's gear in softball practice

Level of Court: Supreme Court, Appellate Division
Date/State: 1990/New York
Decision: Plaintiff/Affirmed

The plaintiff was injured when struck in the face by a softball while catching during an indoor pitching practice for her softball team at the high school gymnasium. The school district requested the trial court for a summary judgment to dismiss the case. The trial court denied the request and the school district appealed. The Appellate Court held that genuine issues of fact existed which required a jury trial on the defendant's alleged negligence in failing to use reasonable care in supervising a girls' softball practice session and in failing to provide proper protective equipment to the plaintiff.

In making its ruling, the court reviewed the record which indicated that after demonstrating proper softball pitching technique, including "the windmill and slingshot high velocity pitches," the pitchers were instructed to begin pitching. The plaintiff, who normally played second base, had volunteered to be one of the catchers. The pitchers were throwing from 40 feet away. Although two sets of protective equipment, including face masks, were present in the gymnasium, no one was instructed or required to use them. A handbook issued by the State Athletic Association stated that "catchers playing modified softball are to wear a helmet and mask and that any player warming up a pitcher, on or off the field, shall wear protective equipment." Expert testimony was presented that indicated the failure to provide or require the use of a face mask constituted a breach of sound coaching practice.

Note. Protective equipment which is readily available for use by athletic teams is frequently not made available to students in physical education classes. Softball is a prime example. Even though physical education classes typically use a much softer ball than that used by athletic teams, the potential for injury still exists, especially as a result of foul tips. Every attempt should be made to provide students with the protective gear which is common to the activities being taught.

Sutphen v. Benthian and the Vernon Township Board of Education
397 A. 2d 709

> Issue: Equipment — Lack of protective equipment
> in floor hockey

Level of Court: Superior Court, Appellate Division
Date/State: 1979/New Jersey
Decision: Dismissed/Reversed

The plaintiff, a tenth grade student, was struck in the eye by a hockey puck while playing floor hockey in his physical education class. The accident resulted in a retinal detachment and eventual removal of the eye. The plaintiff and plaintiff's father sued the physical education teacher and the school district alleging negligence in requiring him to participate in the hockey game "with an excessive number of players on each team, in a playing area that was too small for the purpose, and without providing him with, and requiring him to use, proper protective equipment during the contest." The following facts were not disputed in this case:

1. School authorities were aware, from the time the plaintiff entered kindergarten, that he had a sight deficiency in his right eye.
2. The gym, at the time of the accident, was divided in half with the hockey game being played on one-half of the court.
3. No protective equipment for the facial areas or the eyes were provided and while safety glasses were available if requested, no such request was made by the plaintiff.

The defendants moved for summary judgment at the trial court, contending they were immune from liability under the New Jersey Tort Claims Act and that they owed no duty to the plaintiff. Their claim to immunity was based on assertions that their acts were discretionary and thus immune from suit. The trial court granted summary judgment for the defendants.

The Appellate Court reversed the trial court judgment and remanded the case for trial. The court ruled that the conduct of the teacher was clearly not the type of "high-level policy decision" addressed by the section of the tort claims act dealing with discretionary duties. In holding the summary judgment to be entirely unwarranted, the Appellate Court stated the case clearly presented several questions of fact for determination by a jury, including:

1. Whether the floor hockey game sponsored by the defendants was an activity having more than the basic elements of risk, due to the nature of the game;
2. Whether participation in this activity required the wearing of protective equipment;
3. Whether, in the circumstances, the supervision provided was adequate;
4. Whether defendants were negligent in leaving to the plaintiff the decision to wear or not to wear a face mask and safety glasses;

5. Whether the defendants were negligent in allowing the plaintiff, who they knew had defective vision in his right eye, to participate in a potentially dangerous activity without protective equipment;
6. Whether defendants had given the plaintiff adequate prior instruction in the skills and dangers of floor hockey; and
7. Whether defendants were negligent in organizing and sponsoring the floor hockey game to be played in a small area of the gym and with an excess number of players on each team.

The court dismissed the defendant's claim that no duty was owed, asserting that such a claim was without any merit.

Berman v. Philadelphia Board of Education
456 A. 2d 545

Issue: Equipment — Lack of mouth guards and other safety equipment in hockey

---

Level of Court: Superior Court
Date/State: 1983/Pennsylvania
Decision: Plaintiff/Affirmed

The plaintiff, an 11-year-old fifth grade student, turned out for an after school intramural hockey program run by the physical education specialist. During the course of a game, the plaintiff faced an opposing player who made a backhand shot. In making his shot, the opposing player's follow-through motion caused the blade of the hockey stick to hit the plaintiff in the mouth. As a result of being struck, the plaintiff had five teeth severed, causing severe pain and extensive dental treatment. Plaintiff brought action against the school board for negligence based on their failure to provide necessary equipment. The court found for the plaintiff, awarding $83,190 to the child and $1,810 for the parents.

The school board appealed on two grounds. First, they claimed there was insufficient evidence to support a finding of negligence based on the fact that the Amateur Hockey Association of the United States had no regulations requiring mouth guards for participants of amateur ice or floor hockey. The school board contended, therefore, that no standard of care was established upon which a finding of negligence could stand and that without a regulation to the contrary, the teacher was not required to furnish mouth guards. They contended that the teacher's general instructions, officiating of the games and calling of penalties were sufficient actions to satisfy a reasonable standard of care. The school board's second contention in appealing the trial court decision was that the plaintiff assumed the risk and was contributorily negligent.

Testimony showed that the physical education teacher was well aware of the potential for mouth injuries and had, in fact, requested the purchase of safety equipment two or three times during the program's first year, but to no avail. Testimony showed that students were instructed at the beginning of every season that slapshots, raising the hockey sticks above the waist and checking were prohibited. Students were equipped with hockey sticks composed of wooden shafts and plastic blades but no helmets, face masks, mouth guards, shin guards or gloves were provided.

The Superior Court ruled that the duty to provide for the safety and welfare of students participating in the hockey program was breached by the school board. Notwithstanding the fact that there were no rules or regulations requiring mouth guards in effect at the time of the accident, the instructor was well aware of the potential for mouth injuries and had requested the board for appropriate safety equipment.

The court noted that an 11-year-old has a rebuttable presumption of being incapable of contributory negligence. Pennsylvania requires that any rebuttal of this presumption must review the child's conduct "in light of the behavior of [children] of similar age, intelligence and experience." Noting that the plaintiff's only experience and knowledge of hockey was obtained in the school program and that no previous serious injuries had occurred in the program, the court ruled the plaintiff incapable of contributory negligence.

As to assumption of risk, the court ruled that by reason of his young age and lack of intelligence, experience and information, the plaintiff did not appreciate the dangers of floor hockey. On the basis of the above arguments, the Superior Court affirmed the trial court judgment of negligence.

Lentz v. Morris
372 S.E. 2d 608

Issue: Lack of protective gear — Tackle football in physical education

Level of Court: State Supreme Court
Date/State: 1985/Virginia
Decision: Defendant/Affirmed with dissent

The plaintiff was injured while playing tackle football during class without wearing any protective equipment. Suit was brought alleging that the physical education teacher was negligent for allowing the game to be played without protective gear when he knew or should have known that the game posed a danger to the participants. The suit also alleged negligent supervision in allowing the plaintiff to be tackled with "great force and violence," thereby causing his injuries. The trial court ruled in favor of the defendants on the grounds of governmental immunity.

On appeal, the plaintiff contended that the trial court erred in ruling the teacher immune from suit. The plaintiff's contention was based on two previous decisions by the Virginia Supreme Court. In Crabbe v. School Board and Albrite, 164 S.E. 2d 639 (1968), the Supreme Court ruled that governmental immunity of school districts did not extend to teachers in the performance of their duties. The court held that the teachers are liable for their own acts of negligence. The Supreme Court upheld this decision 11 years later in Short v. Griffits, 255 S.E. 2d 479 (1979) where the court ruled that an athletic director, baseball coach, and buildings and grounds supervisor did not enjoy immunity in a suit by a student who was injured when he fell on broken glass while running laps on the school track.

In the current case, the Supreme Court upheld the trial court decision of immunity, thereby overruling the two decisions cited by the plaintiff. In making its decision, the court relied on its decision in Messina v. Burden, 321 S.E. 2d 657 (1984). In Messina, the court reviewed its prior decisions on governmental immunity which arose from diverse factual situations and outlined a four-part test to be used in determining individual entitlement to immunity. The four factors to be considered in making the determination are:

1. "The nature of the function the employee performs;
2. The extent of the government entity's interest and involvement in the function;
3. The degree of control and direction exercised by the governmental entity over the employee; and
4. Whether the alleged wrongful act involved the exercise of judgment and discretion."

The court ruled in the present case that the teacher was performing an important public function as a school teacher and that the school district had both official interest and direct involvement in the instruction and supervision of students, and that the district does in fact exercise control and direction over the teacher through the school principal. The court also held that a teacher's supervision and control of a physical education class, including the decision as to what equipment is to be worn by student participants, involves the exercise of judgment and discretion. The lower court decision was affirmed.

Justice Stephenson dissented. In his dissent, Justice Stephenson stated that both the Crabbe and Short unanimous decisions represented 20 years of established law and the fact that the state legislature never enacted any legislation to overrule the Crabbe decision indicated that the legislature considered the Crabbe decision to be sound public policy.

Note. This case was decided solely on the basis of the immunity issue. In any jurisdiction where a school district is not cloaked in immunity, it would be very difficult to defend a decision to involve students in a game which involves tackling and where no protective equipment is provided. Prudent practice requires the provision of reasonable safety equipment in any activity which demands it whether it is football, wrestling, softball, or any other activity where protective equipment is needed to effectively reduce the risk of student injury.

Locilento v. John A. Coleman Catholic High School
523 N.Y.S. 2d 198

Issue: Lack of protective equipment and implied assumption
of risk — Intramural tackle football

Level of Court: Supreme Court, Appellate Division
Date/State: 1987/New York
Decision: Plaintiff/Affirmed

The plaintiff received shoulder injuries as a result of tackling another student during an annual intramural game of tackle football in which no protective equipment was provided. The plaintiff brought suit charging the school with negligence in its supervision of the game and in failing to provide the necessary safety equipment and training for the game. The trial court denied the school district's motion for dismissal and the jury returned a verdict for the plaintiff which held the school 60 percent negligent.

On appeal, the district argued that the trial court erred in not dismissing the case for a failure to adequately establish the proximate cause of the injury. The court upheld the lower court finding on causation.

The court noted that while it could not guarantee that the injury would not have occurred if the plaintiff had worn shoulder pads, it could clearly hold that the risk of this type of injury was substantially enhanced with the absence of the protective gear. The court also ruled against the district claim of nonliability based upon the plaintiff's assumption of risk.

The court ruled that implied assumption of risk does not act as a total bar to recovery in New York and that any assumption of risk should be considered when apportioning the liability of a defendant and the plaintiff. The court held there was no evidence that the trial court had erred in its apportionment of damages.

Ausmus v. Board of Education, City of Chicago
508 N.E. 2d 298

Issue: Failure to provide safe equipment — Bat too large
and lack of catcher's gear

Level of Court: Court of Appeals
Date/State: 1987/Illinois
Decision: Defendant/Reversed and remanded

The plaintiff, a third grade elementary student, was injured when struck in the face by a wooden bat swung by a female classmate during a softball game in their physical education class. Suit was filed against the school board and the physical education teacher. The plaintiff charged negligence for providing unsafe equipment by (1) furnishing class members with a regulation size and weight wooden bat which was too heavy to be safely held and swung by children of the age and experience of the plaintiff, (2) failing to provide less dangerous equipment such as a plastic bat, lighter wooden bat, or an aluminum bat, (3) failing to provide a helmet or face mask to protect the child acting as catcher, (4) failing to provide a backstop or other markings to indicate the areas which were safe for batting and catching, and (5) failing to provide adequate medical and first aid equipment for use by school personnel in attending to injuries.

The trial court granted the board's motion for dismissal on the grounds that Illinois state law confers upon districts and teachers the status of "in loco parentis," which grants them the same status as parents and like parents makes them liable only for willful and wanton misconduct and not mere negligence.

On appeal, the Appellate Court of Illinois reversed the dismissal and remanded the case for jury consideration. In so ruling, the court held that the "in loco parentis immunity" of a school district and its employees does not extend to the failure to provide safe equipment and that the failure to furnish equipment does not absolve any liability for failure to provide effective equipment. The court held that school districts have an affirmative duty to furnish equipment to prevent serious injuries.

Santee v. Orleans Parish School Board
430 So. 2d 254

Issue: Equipment dangerous when not used for intended purpose

Level of Court: Court of Appeals
Date/State: 1983/Louisiana
Decision: Plaintiff/Affirmed

The plaintiff was eight years old at the time of the accident and was playing jacks at lunch recess on the school playground. Two supervisors plus the principal were on playground duty and were responsible for supervising 200 children in two separate areas, one on each side of the school building. While the plaintiff was playing jacks, several other girls were rolling a stand used as a volleyball standard and tetherball pole around the playground. The standard consisted of a pole imbedded in a large tire filled with concrete. When the girls saw the principal coming, they ran away and the standard rolled over the plaintiff's fingers.

Trial testimony indicated there had been a previous problem with students playing with the standards. The principal recognized the danger posed and had threatened a three-day suspension for anyone caught playing with them. On the day of the accident, the principal saw the girls rolling the standard and was in the process of sneaking up on them when the plaintiff's fingers were injured. The trial court found the district negligent and awarded damages.

The Court of Appeals upheld the lower court finding of negligence based on inadequate supervision and failure of the school to make the equipment inaccessible to students for anything other than the intended purpose. The court ruled that while the stands were not inherently dangerous, their misuse by students and the principal's knowledge regarding their continued misuse and the risk of injury required that measures be taken to make the standards inaccessible to the students. The court further held that three supervisors for 200 children in completely separate areas of the school grounds was inadequate. The court took note of the fact that the principal, upon noticing the prohibited activity, was more concerned about sneaking up on and catching the guilty girls than putting an immediate stop to what he recognized as a dangerous activity.

Cappel v. Board of Education,
Union Free School District No. 4, Northport
337 N.Y.S. 2d 836

Issue: Attractive nuisance — Field hockey goal cage

Level of Court: Supreme Court, Appellate Division
Date/State: 1972/New York
Decision: Defendant/Reversed and new trial granted

The plaintiff, five years of age, was injured while playing on a school playground when other children attempted to lift a field hockey goal cage and dropped it. Evidence showed that the cage was constructed of heavy galvanized steel pipe, was about seven feet tall and twelve feet wide, was located in the middle of the playing field of a junior high school where neighborhood children were welcome to play, and was not fastened to the ground in any way. Testimony indicated that the cage was easily tipped over. On the day of the accident, the children had previously tipped the cage over prior to attempting to lift it.

The trial court dismissed the complaint at the end of the plaintiff's case. The Supreme Court reversed this decision and ordered a new trial. In granting the new trial, the court held that the evidence was sufficient for presentation of the case to the jury. The court held that the school district owed a duty to keep the school grounds in a reasonably safe condition. Invoking some of the principles of the doctrine of attractive nuisance, the court ruled the duty of the district included consideration of the known propensities of children to climb about and play. The court held that in this case, the duty owed to children who could reasonably be anticipated to come onto the school grounds and play on the cage was greater than that owing to a mere licensee.

Note. As school playgrounds are held open to the public, a child coming onto the premises to play would be an invitee rather than a trespasser. The doctrine of attractive nuisance applies to child trespassers only. The duty owed to the plaintiff in this case was in fact greater than that owed to a licensee but the attractive nuisance doctrine does not apply. The highest standard of care is owed to the invitee, one who is on the premises at the express or implied invitation of the school. With respect to invitees, schools have the duty to inspect and discover dangerous natural or artificial conditions as well as dangerous activities on the premises. Depending on the danger involved, the school must either warn the invitee or make the condition or activity safe.

The same problem presented by this case exists relative to metal soccer goal posts. While weighing nearly 600 pounds, they can easily be tipped over by a half dozen students. Any inspection of these goals would indicate that it is a common occurrence for these goals to be tipped over. When tipped over, students often stand and bounce on the top crossbar. This accounts for the large number of soccer goals on school fields with bent upper crossbars. These goals can easily be temporarily anchored to the ground. A 1-2 inch section of pipe welded to the bottom of the left and right back corners of the goal, with a two foot length of steel re-bar driven through the pipe and into the ground will keep the goals from being tipped over. District maintainence can easily pull up the re-bar with either the lift on their mowers or with a tractor bucket. The goals can be relocated if desired.

Fuehrer v. Board of Education of the Westerville City School District
574 N.E. 2d 448

Issue: Soccer goal falls on student

Level of Court: Supreme Court
Date/State: 1991/Ohio
Decision: Defendant/Affirmed

The plaintiff, the mother of a 14-year-old high school student, brought suit against the school district as a result of fatal injuries suffered by her son when a metal goal post fell on him. Trial court evidence indicated that her son and four companions entered the school property after school hours and began playing with the metal soccer goal post. The boys had tipped over the goal post and were attempting to upright it when it slipped and fell on the boy's head. The district claimed that the boys were "recreational users" and that the district was, therefore, immune to suit under the state recreational user statute. The district further claimed that even if not recreational users, the boys were licensees at best and that as licensees, the board owed no duty to warn them of the dangers of the goal posts. The plaintiff charged that the district was negligent in not warning the boys of the dangers posed by the soccer goals. The trial court approved the district's motion for summary judgment and the plaintiff appealed.

The Court of Appeals upheld the summary judgment ruling stating that while the boys were not recreational users, they were licensees. The court held that as licensees, the boys were not owed a duty by the district to warn or protect them from the dangers of the goal post. The plaintiff appealed once again.

The Supreme Court upheld the Court of Appeals decision. The court affirmed the holding that the boys were not recreational users and that the district was, therefore, not immune to suit. The court held that the boys were licensees and that the district owed them no duty "except to refrain from wantonly or willfully injuring them, and to exercise ordinary care after discovering them in peril." The court ruled that failing to warn the boys of the danger posed by the goal post did not constitute wanton and willful conduct and that the district was, therefore, not liable for the boy's death.

Note. The court in this case ruled the boys were licensees and that no duty existed to warn them of the dangers posed by the goal post. Most jurisdictions have held individuals on school playgrounds to be invitees as the playgrounds are clearly held open to the public. In either case, districts are not free to maintain dangerous conditions on their property of which they have constructive knowledge or notice. Soccer goals are commonly tipped over by students as was done by the deceased and his friends. School districts would be prudent to either permanently or temporarily secure these goals to the ground.

Gibbons v. Orleans Parish School Board
391 So. 2d 976

Issue: Attractive nuisance, inadequate supervision

Level of Court: Court of Appeals
Date/State: 1980/Louisiana
Decision: Plaintiff/Affirmed

A six-year-old student received injuries requiring 29 stitches in her thigh as a result of sliding down a tetherball pole which had a screw which protruded one and one-half inches. Trial evidence indicated that the girl began playing on the monkey bars and when she got to the end she grabbed onto the tetherball pole which was located right next to the monkey bars. At the time of the accident, one supervisor was on duty. Testimony indicated that her responsibilities at the time included supervising the unloading of the school buses, supervising the playground which had over 150 students on it, and overseeing students in the school basement. The trial court found the tetherball pole to be an "attractive nuisance" and the supervision of the playground inadequate. The plaintiff was awarded $7,500 in damages.

On appeal, the Court of Appeals held that the tetherball pole in proper use and without the protruding screw would not be deemed dangerous but it became a dangerous instrumentality when placed next to the monkey bars with a screw protruding from it. The pole provided a natural inclination for a child to move from the monkey bars to the pole and to slide to the ground. The court judged the tetherball pole in its condition and location to constitute a dangerous piece of equipment which the district negligently allowed to exist. The court also ruled that the evidence clearly supported a finding of negligent supervision. The court stated that adequate supervision was virtually impossible where the supervisor was required to supervise a large number of students in more than one location.

Note: The student in this case was not a trespasser and the attractive nuisance doctrine does not apply. Because of the natural tendency of children to move from the monkey bars to the tetherball pole, however, the placement of the equipment in this case was ruled negligent.

Jastram v. Lake Villa School District 41
549 N.E. 2d 9

Issue: Fall from monkey bars — Governmental immunity

Level of Court: District Court of Appeals
Date/State: 1989/Illinois
Decision: Defendant/Reversed

The plaintiff received injuries as a result of a fall from the monkey bars during recess on the school playground. Suit was filed charging the district with negligence in failing to adequately supervise, providing a dangerous climbing apparatus, failing to provide a safe place for recess, dangerously constructing a climbing apparatus and placing it on a hard surface, and failing to have a responsible adult on the playground. The plaintiff also charged that the district was guilty of willful and wanton misconduct. The trial court granted the district motion for summary judgment based on its claims of governmental immunity.

On appeal, the Court of Appeals reversed the lower court decision and the summary judgment. The court ruled that under Illinois law, governmental immunity does not extend to the provision of equipment or the maintenance of school premises. The court also held that immunity only applies to situations arising out of the student-teacher relationship and protects teachers in the carrying out of their normal duties such as supervision and instruction.

At the time of the accident, Illinois law only granted this immunity to certified staff. Noncertified staff were held, at the time, to be liable up to the limits of insurance coverage. Because the recess in question was supervised by two noncertified adults, the district could not claim immunity with respect to the supervision of the playground.

Note. Since this accident, Illinois law has been modified and insurance companies are now able to claim immunity for the actions of a public entity which enjoy immunity under the provisions of the Tort Claims Act.

Pell v. Victor J. Andrew High School and AMF, Inc.
462 N.E. 2d 858

> Issue: Equipment — Safety warnings not visible and lack of
> safety harness for gymnastics

Level of Court: State Appellate Court
Date/State: 1984/Illinois
Decision: Plaintiff/Affirmed

The plaintiff, a high school student, was permanently paralyzed when she severed her spinal cord as a result of a fall during the performance of a somersault off of a mini-tramp during her physical education class.   The plaintiff filed suit against the school district, the high school, and the manufacturer of the mini-tramp, AMF, Inc.

Evidence and testimony showed that the mini-tramp was sold to the school district with a heat-laminated caution label attached to the bed which cautioned against misuse or abuse of the equipment and requested users to carefully read all instructions, inspect before using, and replace any worn, defective or missing parts. The label further cautioned of the dangers of activities involving motion or height, use by untrained or unqualified participants, and unsupervised use. When the mini-tramp was assembled by a faculty member of the school, the bed was placed so that the warning label was facing down. Printed warnings on the frame were covered by frame pads.

The plaintiff testified she took a few running steps up to the mini-tramp, jumped onto the bed and began a somersault. Midway through her somersault, she felt a sharp pain in her knee and was unable to properly complete the skill and collapsed onto a nearby mat. Two instructors were present at the time of the accident with the closest one observing the somersault from a distance of ten feet away. No safety harness or spotter was used.

The plaintiff settled out of court with the school district for $1.6 million and the trial court found for the plaintiff in her case against AMF and awarded damages of $3.4 million. AMF appealed on a number of grounds. The Appellate Court ruled that warnings must be adequate to perform their intended function. The court stated that the warnings could be judged inadequate if they do not specify the risk presented by the apparatus, they are inconsistent with how the apparatus would be used, if they do not provide the reason for the warning, or if they do not reach the foreseeable users. The court ruled that the evidence was sufficient to warrant a jury conclusion that the warnings were ineffective. In so ruling, the court stated:

1. "The warnings did not specify the risk of severe spinal cord injury which could result in permanent paralysis if somersaulting off the mini-tramp without a spotter or safety harness ...
2. The warnings were inadequate because their location was inconsistent with equipment's use ...
3. AMF was familiar with recommendations by the [United States Gymnastics Safety] Association that warning labels should explain the reason for the warning and be clearly visible to a mini-tramp user ..."

The Appellate Court ruled against AMF's defense of contributory negligence stating it is not available as a defense in strict liability tort action. It did note that "comparative fault is applicable to strict liability cases but only insofar as the defenses of misuse and assumption of risk are concerned." Comparative fault will not bar recovery but will operate to reduce the plaintiff's recovery by their degree of fault.

The court found no sufficient evidence to support either misuse or assumption of risk on the part of the plaintiff. The trial court's determination of negligence on the part of AMF was affirmed.

Short v. Griffitts
255 S.E. 2d 479

Issue: Maintenance of grounds — Broken glass on track

Level of Court: State Supreme Court
Date/State: 1979/Virginia
Decision: Defendant/Reversed and remanded

The plaintiff brought action against the county school board, athletic director, baseball coach and the buildings and grounds supervisor for injuries sustained when he fell on broken glass while running laps on the school track. The plaintiff alleged that the "individual defendants had a duty to establish procedures for the maintenance of the track and to supervise and instruct the custodial staff of the school to insure that the premises were maintained in a safe condition." The plaintiff alleged that the defendants breached this duty by failing to inspect the premises, failing to discover the dangerous condition present on the track and failing to warn the plaintiff of the dangerous condition.

The trial court sustained the defendant's plea of sovereign immunity and dismissed the case. On appeal, the Supreme Court held that the issues of duty, breach of duty and proximate cause were all issues of fact and as such were questions for the jury. The Supreme Court limited its decision to the issue of sovereign immunity. The court ruled that while the school board was immune to liability, the athletic director, coach and supervisor of buildings and grounds could not assert sovereign immunity as a defense. The holding of the trial court was reversed and the case remanded for trial.

The holding of the court on the application of immunity to the individual teachers was overruled six years later in the case of Lentz v. Morris, in which the Supreme Court ruled that the sovereign immunity of school districts is also extended to teachers employed by the district.

Brock v. Rockridge Community Unit District 300
539 N.E. 2d 445

Issue: Dangerous grounds — Uneven surface of playing field

Level of Court: State Court of Appeals
Date/State: 1989/Illinois
Decision: Defendant/Affirmed

The plaintiff was injured while playing touch football during his physical education class when another participant stepped on an uneven portion of the playing field, lost his balance, and fell into him. The plaintiff filed suit against the district charging negligence in "failing to keep the playing field in a reasonably safe condition, negligently requiring students to use an unreasonably dangerous playing field, and failing to warn of the dangerous contours of the playing field."

The trial court dismissed the complaint on the grounds of governmental immunity but allowed the plaintiff to file an amended complaint. The plaintiff's amended complaint reduced the allegations of negligence to a failure to keep the premises safe and a failure to warn of dangerous conditions. The amended complaint was dismissed for failing to state a cause of action.

On appeal, the Court of Appeals held that the dismissal of the orginal complaint as well as the amended complaint were proper. The court held that the issue at hand in the original complaint was really one involving the supervision of student activities and was, therefore, immune to suit under the state tort claims act. The appellate court ruled that the premise liability exception to liability could not be applied to the facts presented in this case.

Snyder v. Morristown Central School District
563 N.Y.S. 2d 258

Issue: Playing on wet, muddy field

Level of Court: Supreme Court, Appellate Division
Date/State: 1990/New York
Decision: Defendant/Affirmed

The plaintiff injured her knee while participating in a coeducational touch football game in her eighth grade physical education class which was conducted outside during inclement weather on a wet, muddy field. The plaintiff alleged that the school was negligent in conducting the activity on the wet and muddy field and in organizing and conducting a coeducational game where the boys were quicker, stronger, and larger than the girls.

Evidence indicated that the plaintiff lost her footing when she turned to tag a ball carrier. As she fell, one of her own team mates stepped on her instep causing a twisting injury to her knee. The court entered a judgment in favor of the defendant holding that while the wet playing surface may have contributed to the plaintiff's slip, it did not form an adequate basis to assign liability to the school district for playing a game of touch football on a wet field.

The court noted that the plaintiff's fall was not the result of contact with one of the male players and, therefore, no causal relation existed between the injury and the participation of the male players.

Note. Where contact does become a factor in a given activity, consideration needs to be given to matching students for competition. It is not uncommon to see the division made according to sex. This is an inadequate as well as sexist approach to the problem. Consideration should be given to age, size, skill level, and experience when making any decision on how to fairly and safely match students for competition or class play.

Sears v. City of Springhill
303 So. 2d 602

Issue: Unsafe grounds — Open ditch on school grounds

Level of Court: State Court of Appeals
Date/State: 1974/Louisiana
Decision: Plaintiff/Affirmed

During lunch recess, the plaintiff, a 12-year-old student, broke his leg when he fell into an open ditch on the school grounds while playing tag football. Evidence showed that the accident happened within a few days after school opened and that the plaintiff was new to the school. Students were playing on a field approved for such use.

The testimony showed that the plaintiff, running full speed to tag the receiver, was unable to stop after tagging the receiver and fell into the ditch. Evidence indicated the ditch was anywhere from 5-10 feet deep in that area of the school grounds and was at least partially concealed by weeds and grass. There were no barriers nor any posted warnings. While the teacher in charge testified verbal warnings about the ditch had been given on previous occasions, she was unsure as to whether the injured plaintiff was present when the warnings were given.

The trial court awarded the plaintiff $5,000 in damages and the district appealed. The Court of Appeals ruled there was no error in the conclusions of the trial court that found the school district was negligent in permitting the ditch to remain unguarded and without barriers at the edge of the playground and that the negligence of the district was the proximate cause of the plaintiff's injuries.

The court found no merit in the defendant's plea of contributory negligence as it was evident that the plaintiff knew of neither the existence of the ditch nor the dangerous condition of the ditch and the tall grass and weeds which were allowed by the district to remain. The decision of the lower court was affirmed.

Note. This case is one of many that points out the need to assure that all students receive appropriate and necessary safety instructions. Attention needs to be given to delivering these instructions and warnings to students who were either absent the day they were initially presented or who enrolled in the class after the instructions were given.

Massie v. Pearson
729 S.W. 2d 448

Issue: Lack of ground fault interrupter on whirlpool modified by coach

Level of Court: Court of Appeals
Date/State: 1987/Kentucky
Decision: Defendant/Affirmed in part, reversed in part

The plaintiff brought a wrongful death suit against five construction defendants and the high school football coach as a result of the electrocution of her son in a whirlpool located within the athletic facilities of the school. Trial evidence established that the newly built school, 12 years old at the time of the accident, had passed inspection for its compliance with the 1965 National Electric Code in effect at the time construction was completed. It was also shown that four years after completion of the building, the school purchased a portable one-person stainless steel whirlpool. The newly hired football coach constructed a concrete block pool supplied with water from a shower and used the agitator and the control panel from the old stainless steel pool. The new pool was powered by a cord which ran to the control panel which was in turn connected to an electrical outlet in another room. The accident occurred as the plaintiff and another boy used the whirlpool after a baseball game. Evidence at trial supported that there were at least three faulty wiring conditions existing in the whirlpool component, the control panel was plugged into an improperly grounded outlet in violation of the 1965 electrial code in effect when the building was constructed, and there was no ground fault interrupter as required by the 1975 electric code in effect at the time the football coach modified the whirlpool.

The construction defendants filed for and were granted summary judgment based on a five year statute of limitations provision which provided that suit could not be brought for damages which occur more than five years after completion of construction. The trial court also granted summary judgment in the case against the football coach. The plaintiff appealed the lower court ruling while charging the five year statute of limitations provision was unconstitutional and that she was entitled to a directed verdict against the football coach.

The Court of Appeals, while ruling the statute was unconstitutional, held that the plaintiff could not benefit from this finding because of a number of procedural errors or omissions on her part. The dismissal against the construction defendants was, therefore, upheld.

The court went on to state that even if she were able to benefit from the unconstitutionality of the statute of limitation provision, the claim against the construction defendants would have failed anyway in that the evidence would not support that their negligence, if any, was a substantial factor in the boy's death. The court held even though the electrical outlet was improperly grounded, no electrocution would have occurred had a ground fault interruptor been installed according to code when the whirlpool was modified 12 years later. The court ruled that the coach was negligent as a matter of law for not installing the ground fault interruptor and that the plaintiff was entitled to a directed verdict against the coach.

While upholding the summary judgment for the construction defendants, the Court of Appeals reversed the dismissal against the coach and remanded the case against the coach to the trial court for the determination of damages.

Wilkinson v. Hartford Accident and Indemnity Company
411 So. 2d 22

Issue: Facilities — Nonsafety glass in gym area

Level of Court: State Supreme Court
Date/State: 1982/Louisiana
Decision: Defendant/Affirmed/Reversed

The plaintiff's son, then a 12-year-old seventh grader, was injured when he fell through a plate glass window in the lobby outside of the gymnasium. On the day of the accident, the physical education class was involved in relay races on the east half of the basketball court, the side nearest to the lobby. The class was divided into six teams of five with two teams competing at a time. At the conclusion of each race, the boys were instructed to sit along the east wall of the gym and await their next turn. The boys were permitted to go to the lobby to get water at the drinking fountains but were instructed not to linger or engage in horseplay. Following one of the races, the plaintiff's son, David, and the other members of his team went to the lobby to get a drink. While there, they decided to have David and another boy race to determine the order in which they would compete in the next relay. They were to race from the north water fountain to the south glass panel and back. There was a floor-to-ceiling glass panel at each end of the lobby. During their race, David pushed off the glass panel with both hands as he attempted to turn. He fell through the glass panel as it broke and he suffered multiple cuts on his arms and legs and was bleeding severely. The physical education teacher administered first aid and David was taken to the hospital for further treatment.

The plaintiff filed suit on behalf of his injured son against the physical education teacher and school district for negligence. Evidence showed that a nonsafety glass panel at the other end of the lobby, identical to that through which the plaintiff's son crashed, had been broken several years previously when a visiting coach walked into it. It has been replaced with safety glass.

The trial court rendered judgment for the defendant. In dismissing the plaintiff's suit, the court stated that there was no finding of negligence against the physical education teacher and that although negligence on the part of the school district was shown, the plaintiff was denied recovery due to the contributory negligence of the injured boy. The Court of Appeals affirmed the trial court decision.

The Supreme Court framed the issues as whether the physical education teacher was negligent in his supervision of the class and/ or the school board in maintaining a plate glass window in the lobby of the gym and if either or both were negligent, whether plaintiff's action is barred by the contributory negligence of the injured boy. The court supported the finding of the lower courts of no negligence on the part of the physical education teacher. As to the school board, the court ruled that the board had actual and constructive knowledge that the maintenance of plate glass in the lobby of the gym was dangerous and represented an unreasonable hazard to the children under its supervision. The board was, therefore, held liable. The court noted that in determining the contributory negligence of a 12-year-old boy, his conduct must be evaluated on the basis of his "maturity and capacity to evaluate circumstances and that he must only exercise the care expected of his age, intelligence and experience."

The court ruled that the plaintiff's son was not contributorily negligent, stating that the race in the lobby was merely an extension of the races being conducted in the gym, the conduct of the injured boy was normal under the circumstances, and that the boy had no way of knowing that the glass panel contained plate glass rather than safety glass. The court ordered the case remanded to the Court of Appeals for the assignment of damages. On remand, the Court of Appeals awarded $20,560 in total damages.

Driscol v. Delphi Community School Corporation
290 N.E. 2d 769

Issue: Inadequate locker room facilities

Level of Court: State Court of Appeals
Date/State: 1972/Indiana
Decision: Defendant/Affirmed

The plaintiff, a high school student, was injured as a result of falling while running to shower after class. The evidence indicated that a boys and girls class shared a gym with 45 girls in the girls class. The two classes were separated by a canvas curtain. Physical education classes were 55 minutes in length with five minutes allowed for passing between classes. Activity was normally stopped five minutes prior to the end of the period to allow time for the students to undress, shower, dress, comb their hair and exit for their next class. The girls were required to shower but only six shower stalls, each accommodating two girls, were available, allowing only 12 girls to shower at a time. Being tardy to the next class three times counted against their grade and that they faced disciplinary action if they were not out of gym on time. The locker room was very crowded because of the class size and many girls had to share lockers and to dress in the restroom area of the locker room. When told to leave the gym floor, the girls were required to go around the far end of the curtain and to wait until the boys class was dismissed before crossing the floor to the locker room entrance.

On the day of the accident, the girls teacher dismissed the class in the usual manner. The girls, as usual, began to run toward the curtain. After two or three steps, the plaintiff's feet became entangled with those of another student, causing her to fall with several other girls then piling onto her. The fall broke the plaintiff's left femur and cracked her right elbow. She spent considerable time in both the hospital and home in bed. It was several months before she fully recovered.

The plaintiff brought suit, alleging the teacher and the school district to be negligent for permitting too many girls to be in a physical education class, in failing to provide adequate shower facilities and in failing to provide sufficient time for 45 girls to shower. The trial court granted judgment for the defendants at the conclusion of plaintiff's case and the plaintiff appealed.

The Court of Appeals ruled that no showing was made by the evidence that the girl's gym teacher had anything to do with the fixing of the class size nor did the evidence show who in fact fixed the class size and whether that individual had any practical choice in the matter. The court ruled no liability could be assessed in this case based on class size. The court also held that the evidence failed to show that anyone who might have been held liable under the doctrine of respondeat superior had any power or duty to provide a greater number of shower facilities and that the district was, therefore, not liable for their alleged failure to provide adequate facilities. The court noted that the third contention was the only specification of negligence which might have some support in the evidence.

The court noted the girls felt obligated to run in order to make it to their next class on time and that a reasonable inference existed that the physical education teacher might have, on occasion, been able to release the girls a little earlier to give them additional time to shower and dress. However, the court concluded that it would not be reasonable to assume that her power to increase this time was "limitless." The court stated no evidence was provided regarding state and local policy of imposed activity time requirements. The court clearly stated that it did know a boy's class was in session between the girls and their dressing room and that any attempt to send them prior to the boy's class having been dismissed would involve obvious danger of collisions with members of the other class. The court held that the suggestion of holding the teacher negligent for not subjecting the girls to that hazard in order to avoid the necessity of running would be improper. The court ruled that there were serious doubts as to whether any interpretation of the evidence could suggest that the plaintiff or any of her classmates were subjected to any unreasonable risk of injury. The Court of Appeals found that the trial court did not err in granting judgment for the defendants and the lower court judgment was affirmed.

Note. Physical educators would be prudent to carefully examine the interaction of class size, facility arrangement, class requirements, shower facilities, scheduling and their potential impact on liability of programs. Locker room facilities are perhaps the most dangerous in school buildings and represent a significant liability problem. Even in the above jurisdiction, the outcome may have been different had the girl fallen after entering the locker room facility rather than outside the facility on the gym floor.

Morris v. Orleans Parish School Board
553 So. 2d 427

Issue: Failure to repair leaking drinking fountain

Level of Court: State Supreme Court
Date/State: 1989/Louisiana
Decision: Plaintiff/Reversed/Reversed

A 12-year-old elementary school student was injured when she slipped and fell on wet asphalt underneath and in front of a drinking fountain as she ran to get a drink. She fell on her right hip and after two days of continuing pain was taken to a hospital where she was diagnosed as having a muscle strain. She returned to the hospital two days later as the pain intensified and she began to run a fever and suffered limited motion in her hip. She was diagnosed as having a hip infection and surgery was performed to drain the joint and remove the infected substance. Her wound was left open for two weeks. She was released from the hospital five weeks after surgery and spent two weeks on crutches before she returned to school. She was retained one year in school, had a five-inch scar on her hip, and still experienced pain when she ran.

Suit was brought against the school board for negligently maintaining a dangerous condition on school grounds which caused the plaintiff's injuries. Evidence presented at trial indicated that the drinking fountain leaked and that the school board had received a request to repair worn gaskets on the fountain six months before the accident. The school board received a second request regarding the same fountain two months prior to the plaintiff's accident. This request came from a parent and it was listed as a request for emergency repairs.

In addition to the parent's request, the board also received one from the school custodian three months before the fall after he was unsuccessful in repairing it. He considered the request to be of an emergency nature because of safety concerns. Work on the fountain was not undertaken until two months after the plaintiff's fall.

The trial court awarded $48,538 to the plaintiff in finding the defendants negligent. The Court of Appeals reversed the trial court decision while holding that the plaintiff failed to prove that the fall caused the infection in her hip.

The Supreme Court reviewed the following three issues upon granting a review of the Court of Appeals decision:

1. "Whether the school district was negligent;
2. If so, whether the fall caused the infection in her hip joint; and
3. If so, whether the awarded damages by the trial judge were proper."

The Supreme affirmatively answered the questions to all three issues and reversed the Court of Appeals while reinstating the judgment of the trial court.

Note. This case points out the necessity of making prompt repairs of defective or unsafe equipment and facilities. When defective or unsafe conditions are found to exist, immediate work orders for repair should be submitted. While awaiting repairs, use of the unsafe equipment or facility by students should not be permitted.

Truelove v. Wilson
285 S.E. 2d 556

Issue: Metal goal post falls and kills student

Level of Court: Court of Appeals
Date/State: 1981/Georgia
Decision: Defendant/Affirmed

An elementary school student was fatally injured when a metal soccer goal post fell on her as she was tying her shoe in her physical education class. A wrongful death suit was filed by her parents against the school district and 14 individual defendants charging negligence in the maintenance of a nuisance. The Court of Appeals ruled that the doctrine of sovereign immunity shielded all of the defendants from liability. The court noted that whatever their personal feelings regarding the justness of the doctrine, the members of the court are bound to apply the law as it currently exists.

Note. While all of the discussion in this case centered on the issue of governmental immunity, this case does point out the need to have an ongoing plan of inspection for equipment, grounds, and facilities. Outdoor areas open to the public during nonschool hours and permanent fixtures such as goals which are exposed to both the effects of weather and vandalism need to receive at least a quick visual check on a daily basis before they are used.

Eberhard v. St. Johns Public Schools
473 N.W. 2d 745

Issue: Disrepair of playground basketball hoop

Level of Court: Court of Appeals
Date/State: 1991/Michigan
Decision: Defendant/Affirmed

The plaintiff was injured while playing basketball on his elementary school playground when the basketball hoop fell and struck him. The trial court granted summary judgment for the school district based on governmental immunity. The plaintiff appealed, claiming that the trial court erred in not applying the public building exception to governmental immunity.

The Court of Appeals affirmed the summary judgment of the lower court, holding that the public building exception to governmental immunity relates to dangers presented by the building itself and not to dangers presented on school property adjacent to the building.

Note. While governmental immunity protected the district in this case, school districts need to exercise care in keeping outside facilities and equipment in good repair. Those assigned responsibility for inspecting building facilities and equipment need to conduct regular inspections and make needed repairs before allowing equipment or facilities to be used. Because of the beating that outdoor backboards take from the weather, regular inspection of all hoops is crucial.

Physical educators need to assume some responsibility for this process in those areas in which they have expertise and in which they often conduct their activities. This case is but one more reminder of the need to conduct not only regular detailed inspections of all facilities but quick visual checks of facilities and equipment by a supervisor before turning a group of children loose to play.

Dunne v. Orleans Parish School Board
63 So. 2d 1267

Issue: Facilities — Gym unlocked when not in use

Level of Court: State Supreme Court
Date/State: 1985/Louisiana
Decision: Plaintiff/Affirmed/Reversed

The plaintiff, a nine-year-old boy, attended a dance recital in the auditorium of the high school with his parents. During the time he was there, he wandered out of the auditorium and across the hall into the unlocked and unsupervised gymnasium where three other boys were playing on a set of gymnastic rings. The boys invited the plaintiff to play on the rings and, since they were seven feet off the floor and out of reach of the plaintiff, one of the boys brought over a chair for him to stand on. After standing on the chair and grabbing the rings, one of the boys pulled the plaintiff by his feet back toward the bleachers as far as he could go. Despite the pleas of the plaintiff, the boy released him and the rings swung out as far as they could go at which point the plaintiff "flipped off," falling to the floor and injuring his head and shoulder.

Testimony and evidence during the trial indicated that when not in use, the rings were secured by a separate rope against the wall above the collapsible bleachers, about 12-15 feet off the floor. The evidence did not show who removed the ropes from the secured position. The principal testified that the removal was usually accomplished by use of a pole. Testimony claimed that while all of the outside doors to the gym and the building were kept locked, it was impractical to keep the doors from the gym to the hallway locked because the gym was not only used during the school day for classes, but after hours by athletic teams and community groups as well.

The trial court found for the plaintiff. The Court of Appeals upheld the conclusion of the trial court that had the doors been locked, the accident would not have occurred and that the failure to lock the doors was a cause-in-fact of the accident.

On appeal to the Supreme Court, the court noted that while the unlocked doors may have been a cause-in-fact of the accident, such a finding was not sufficient by itself to assign liability. The Supreme Court framed the critical issue in this case as the duty owed by the school board. The court took notice that no expert testimony was offered indicating that the gymnastic rings were inherently dangerous or represented an unreasonable risk of harm in normal use.

Given the precautions to secure the rings mentioned by the principal, the court ruled that the scope of the board's duty did not encompass the risk that a small child would be enticed by older boys to stand on a chair and grab the rings, which had been removed from their secured position, and then be forced to swing on the rings against his will, an act outside the normal use of the rings.

The Supreme Court, therefore, reversed the Court of Appeals decision and dismissed the plaintiff's action.

Ward v. Community Unit School District No. 220
572 N.E. 2d 986

> Issue: Lack of space between two playing fields

Level of Court: State Court of Appeals
Date/State: 1991/Illinois
Decision: Defendant/Affirmed

The plaintiff, a nine-year-old elementary school student, was injured as a result of a collision with a middle school student. Trial court evidence indicated that the middle school and elementary school were adjacent to one another and that they shared a large playing field area in the back. The large playing area was divided into smaller game areas which were marked off using a permanent substance to designate boundaries. The fields were used by both schools for physical education, intramurals, and athletics. Two of the fields were used for football and soccer and were laid out in an end-to-end fashion. On the day of the plaintiff's accident, he was sitting in the end zone of one of the football fields watching an intramural game of flag football. The adjacent field was being used by a middle school physical education class for a football game. The injury occurred when a middle school student ran through his end zone and into the adjacent field while attempting to catch a football. When the middle school student collided with the plaintiff, he accidentally kicked him in the head causing a depressed skull fracture. From this injury, the plaintiff developed permanent seizures and epilepsy. The plaintiff alleged that the school district was guilty of negligence as well as willful and wanton misconduct in the design and use of the two fields which were almost immediately adjacent to one another. The trial court dismissed the case for failing to state a proper cause of action. This ruling was based on the state statute granting governmental immunity to school districts and their employees. The plaintiff appealed the lower court ruling.

On appeal, the Appellate Court held that the district and its teachers were immune from liability for any alleged negligence in its supervision of the games which were taking place when the injury occurred. The court ruled that the exception to immunity for the use or supplying of defective equipment did not extend to allegedly defective premises created by the physical layout of the playing fields. The court found that even if negligent, no evidence was presented which would support finding the use of the adjacent fields as being willful and wanton misconduct. The court took note that the language of the complaint was very general rather than specifying dimensions and distances. The finding of the lower court was affirmed and the case dismissed.

Note. Despite a favorable ruling for the defendant based upon immunity, this case sounds a clear warning to physical educators, coaches, and administrative staff who have responsibility for overseeing activity programs as well as the development and maintenance of facilities. It is commonly accepted that in the playing of games, students will quite often over-run boundaries. In any game, especially those involving contact, the potential not only for over-running boundaries, but for being pushed or tripped is very real. It is essential that an adequate safety space or buffer zone be provided between all playing areas and between playing areas and permanent structures, walls, or other obstructions. This applies to both indoor and outdoor facilities. Having volleyball, badminton, or basketball courts which share a common sideline presents real safety concerns. Effort should be made to create a safety space between courts and playing areas even if it necessitates cutting down slightly the dimensions of the court or field itself. Always allow as much space as possible between playing boundaries and walls. A minimum of 6-8 feet, depending upon the activity, is recommended. Whenever the clearance beyond boundaries is minimal, walls and permanent obstructions should be padded. Never use a wall as a boundary.

Zawadzki v. Taylor
246 N.W. 2d 161

Issue: Lack of safety net or other safety devise
between tennis courts

Level of Court: Court of Appeals
Date/State: 1976/Michigan
Decision: Defendant/Affirmed

The plaintiff received his injuries as a result of being struck by a tennis ball hit by a player on an adjacent tennis court. Suit was filed against the student who hit the ball as well as the school district. Trial court evidence showed that the plaintiff's physical education class was playing tennis indoors on a floor which was marked out to provide two immediately adjacent courts. The charge against the school district alleged negligence in failing to incorporate into the design and maintenance of the gym adequate nets or other safety devices which would reduce the risk of tennis balls crossing from one court to another. The trial court granted the district's motion for an accelerated judgment in holding that it was immune to suit under the tort claims act.

The Court of Appeals upheld the lower court decision holding that school districts in Michigan are protected from suit by governmental immunity. Michigan statute does provide for several exceptions to immunity. One of these exceptions holds school districts liable for their failure to maintain their facilities in a safe condition. The building exception to public body immunity places a duty on public bodies to prevent dangerous or defective conditions from existing within their facilities. The Court of Appeals agreed with the lower court, however, in finding that the district's failure to erect safety nets or other safety devices between the tennis courts in this case did not properly fall within the intent of the public building exception to immunity. The court found that the injury was not due to any defect in the existing building but allegedly from a failure to provide a piece of safety equipment.

Note. While this case was decided on the issue of immunity, it raises an important issue for athletic directors, maintenance departments, coaches, and teachers. When laying out court or field boundries, whether painting a floor, marking it with floor tape, or lining the field, care needs to be taken to provide a buffer or safety zone between courts or field areas. Sharing of a common boundry line between two or more courts is a dangerous practice. While a buffer zone would most likely not have prevented the accident in this case, it would serve to significantly reduce the risk of injury due to player collisions or from being struck by a racket. Injuries resulting from being struck by rackets are common in all racket sport games while student collisions are common to all activities. Adequate safety zones need to be provided between all courts and beyond all boundary lines.

Braun v. Board of Education of Red Bud Community Unit School District No. 132
502 N.E. 2d 1076

> Issue: Failing to disseminate appropriate information about epileptic student and providing him with dangerous equipment

Level of Court: Court of Appeals
Date/State: 1986/Illinois
Decision: Defendant/Affirmed

The plaintiff received serious injuries when he fell 15 feet from a ladder to the floor while posting names on the scoreboard in the gymnasium in preparation for a basketball game. The plaintiff was the student manager of the basketball team. He was directed by the coach to use a 20 foot extension ladder for the task as the scaffold used for this purpose was in the storage shed. Evidence presented at trial indicated that the boy was both epileptic and hyperactive and had a long history of seizures. His health status was part of his permanent record and was also included on his health record. Testimony indicated he had a seizure a week before the accident and that the basketball coach was told about the seizure. The coach was well aware of the boy's health record as he had engaged in conversations with the parents and knew the boy quite well. The coach was under the impression that medication had the problem under control. On the day of the accident, the plaintiff blacked out and fell to the floor.

Illinois law holds teachers and school districts liable for willful and wanton misconduct. It provides immunity for ordinary negligence except in cases of providing dangerous equipment or maintaining unsafe facilities. The trial court found the teacher and school district not guilty of willful and wanton misconduct but found the district negligent in supplying the plaintiff with dangerous equipment as well as failing to supply safe equipment (scaffold) for the task. The jury, while finding the plaintiff 15 percent contributorily negligent, returned an award of $470,000 for the plaintiff. The trial judge entered a judgment notwithstanding the verdict on behalf of the defendants, and the plaintiff appealed as to all three charges in his original complaint.

The Court of Appeals ruled that the district had not failed to provide appropriate equipment. It held that a scaffold was available but that an employee, acting within a supervisory function, chose not to use it but to use a ladder instead. Because the necessary equipment was available, the decision not to use it in this case was subject to the more stringent liability standard of willful and wanton misconduct. The court held that the coach was not guilty of willful and wanton misconduct in having the plaintiff use a ladder because the coach was under the impression that the plaintiff's condition was under control with medication and the plaintiff gave no indication that he was not to climb ladders. The court ruled that the "plaintiff's recent seizure record as known by the coach or other school personnel was not such that placing him on a ladder could be held as willful and wanton as a matter of law" and, therefore, the jury decision relative to the issue of willful and wanton misconduct had to be upheld.

The plaintiff also contended that the district was guilty of willful and wanton misconduct for failing to disseminate appropriate information relative to his condition. The court reasoned that the verdict of the lower court indicated the jury felt otherwise and that this holding was not erroneous as a matter of law. The Appellate Court held that any failure to disseminate information could not be held to be the proximate cause of the plaintiff's injuries as the basketball coach, by his own testimony, was obviously well aware of the boy's condition and more informed than any other employee of the school.

Justice Kasserman dissented from the majority ruling. In his dissent, he suggested that evidence presented at trial was such that a jury could properly conclude that the district had failed in its duty by not directing the scaffolding to be placed in an accessible location and that the danger posed by using a ladder for the directed task should have been recognized by school officials, particularly in view of the plaintiff's epilepsy. The judge concluded that the district was negligent under the real property exception to immunity and that the jury verdict for the plaintiff on this count of the complaint should be reinstated.

Note. There is a clear responsibility to take into account the physical capabilities and health status of students before requiring their participation in any activity or in assigning them managerial tasks such as the one in this case. While the defense successfully argued that the district's action failed to rise to the willful and wanton standard required for negligence under Illinois law, it is likely that a case of negligence could have been successfully argued in jurisdictions assigning liability for ordinary negligence. It is also conceivable that another court could have found the district's action in this case to constitute willful and wanton misconduct.

Byrd v. Bossier Parish School Board
543 So. 2nd 35

> Issue: Student manager injured while using power machinery

Level of Court: State Court of Appeals
Date/State: 1989/Louisiana
Decision: Defendant/Affirmed/Reversed

The plaintiff, a 14-year-old student athletic manager, suffered severe leg injuries when his leg entered an extractor which he was operating. An extractor is a device which wrings clothes much the same way as the spin cycle on a washing machine. Suit was brought against the manufacturer, the school board, the coach, the principal, and the district director of maintenance.

Evidence at the trial court indicated the plaintiff was a student manager for the basketball team. At the time of the accident, he was washing clothes in preparation for a 5:00 freshman game. The extractor, located in the varsity locker room, was equipped with an automatic braking system activated by a timer. It was also equipped with an interlock lever that could be used to break the electrical circuit and thereby cause the electrical brake to apply. The plaintiff's physical education instructor testified he never personally instructed the plaintiff on the operation of the extractor but had done so with other students; they were given instructions never to raise the lid while the tub was spinning. He also testified that he was aware of a problem with the extractor failing to stop and had communicated that to another coach. The basketball coach testified he instructed two team managers on the operation of the extractor and directed them to instruct the other managers. The plaintiff indicated he was instructed on how to use the machine by one of the two managers and was told to never stick hands or any other part of the body in the machine. There were also signs in the locker room that informed the managers not to open the lid while the tub was spinning.

On the day of the accident, the plaintiff turned off the switch on the extractor and lifted the lid, but the extractor continued to run. He attempted to use the interlock lever to stop the machine but it failed to stop. The plaintiff claims he attempted to use his foot on the lever in order to apply more pressure and climbed on top of the machine to do so and did not remember anything after that. The defendants testified that based on their discussions with the plaintiff they believed he attempted to stop the machine with his foot. As a result of the accident, the plaintiff lost his leg.

The trial court dismissed the case against the manufacturer when it settled with the plaintiff out of court. The court granted motions for directed verdicts in favor of the coach, the principal, and the director of maintenance, but denied the motion for a directed verdict for the school board, and the suit continued. The court found the board negligent through the actions of the plaintiff's physical education teacher on the basis of failing to supervise and instruct the plaintiff on the use of the machine. The court also found the plaintiff to be contributorily negligent, however, and recovery of damages was, therefore, barred.

The plaintiff appealed and the Court of Appeals upheld, with dissent, the trial court finding of contributory negligence on the part of the plaintiff. It held that the plaintiff was aware of the dangers posed but nonetheless consciously undertook a dangerous act. The court then focused on claims by the plaintiff that even if he were contributorily negligent, he should not be barred from recovery because the district violated a state statute which prohibits minors under the age of 16 to be "employed, permitted, or suffered to work ... in, or about, power-driven machinery." The court refused to apply the statute to the educational setting and held that the plaintiff was not employed by the district.

The Court of Appeals granted a rehearing and ruled that the statute in question recognized that minors under the age of 16 might not be able to act prudently in every situation and that this case was such a situation. It ruled that the school board and the manufacturer were joint tortfeasors and that the school board would be held liable for half the assessed damages, to go along with whatever amount the plaintiff settled for with the manufacturer in their out-of-court settlement.

Note. Responsibility for instruction in the use of dangerous equipment should never be delegated to other students. When using any power machinery or dangerous equipment, students should receive personal instruction on that equipment's use by the teacher or coach. After receiving instructions, any use of such equipment by students should be carefully and directly supervised by the teacher or coach in charge. In addition, in regard to another aspect of this case, any equipment which is broken, worn, or malfunctioning should be repaired before allowing its further use, or replaced.

IN SUMMARY

THE REASONABLY PRUDENT PHYSICAL EDUCATOR OR COACH:

1. Regularly inspects equipment, facilities and grounds used by students. Does quick visual check daily with a detailed inspection monthly.

2. Keeps all inspection reports on file.

3. Reports all hazardous facility or grounds conditions immediately and refrains from using hazardous areas until these conditions are remedied.

4. Does not use defective, overly worn or broken equipment.

5. Refrains from using equipment for purposes other than those for which it was intended.

6. Provides all necessary safety equipment in those activities where appropriate such as soccer, hockey, softball, football, and gymnastics.

7. Purchases equipment of high quality; does not supply equipment that is dangerous for its intended use.

8. Does not modify factory purchased equipment.

9. Properly secures and/or stores all equipment when not in use.

10. Does not turn an otherwise safe facility into a dangerous one by improperly arranging equipment and materials for student or athlete use (e.g., placing equipment too close to walls, bleachers or other obstructions or crowding).

11. Instructs students and athletes to also check for common safety hazards involving equipment, facilities and grounds.

12. Posts appropriate warnings and rules relative to equipment and facility use.

13. Is cautious in the use of homemade equipment.

14. Keeps locker rooms clean and orderly.

ADMINISTRATION OF FIRST AID

Physical education and athletic staff should possess an understanding of the injuries common to the activities which they teach and coach as well as the first aid required for those injuries. First aid is temporary emergency care, not treatment. It is important that physical educators and coaches not put themselves in a position of diagnosing or treating injuries and/or illnesses. The immediacy as well as the appropriateness of specific first aid measures are issues which have been dealt with in court. The moving of injured students and athletes is another issue which can raise concerns.

Head injuries represent a special problem for physical education and athletic staff. All too often, teachers and coaches put themselves in a precarious position by not taking head injuries seriously. All head injuries should be considered serious and whenever any doubt exists as to the extent of injury, medical help should be summoned immediately. A common sense look at the cause of the injury should provide some clue as to whether or not immediate medical help is prudent. In any case, parents should be notified of all head injuries, whether they appear serious or not.

Physical education and athletic personnel should assume an active role in helping to develop a detailed building plan for dealing with serious injuries. The plan should be clearly communicated and accessible in written form to all staff and should outline procedures to be followed as well as all staff responsibilities.

Coaches should maintain an accurate team roster which includes both home and parent work phone numbers as well as the phone numbers of emergency contacts. This roster should be in the coaches' possession at all game and practice sessions. Whenever traveling out of town for contests, coaches should have in their possession an emergency treatment authorization form for each athlete. This form should include all pertinent information required when seeking medical treatment. It should include student name, family physician, insurance information, allergies if they exist, current medication being taken, and parents' names and signatures.

Due to the increased opportunity for injuries to occur in the physical education and sport setting, physical education and athletic departments, together with the health services coordinator, should develop guidelines for AIDS prevention. This is not only important for self-protection during the administration of first aid but also to prevent the potential spread of the AIDS virus among other class or team members after injuries have occurred. Wrestling is a prime example of a potential problem area with respect to AIDS.

While charges of improper first aid are not nearly as frequent as those for improper instruction and supervision, the following court cases point to the importance of observing the preceding guidelines.

Mogabgab v. Orleans Parish School Board
239 So. 2d 456

```
Issue:  Improper first aid for heat stroke
```

Level of Court: State Court of Appeals
Date/State: 1970/Louisiana
Decision: Dismissed/Reversed

The parents of a deceased high school student brought a wrongful death suit against the school board, the head and assistant football coaches, the principal, superintendent, insurance company and the supervisor of the health, safety and physical education division.

The plaintiffs alleged negligence in failing to provide all necessary and reasonable safeguards to prevent injury and illness to members of the football team and negligence for improper first aid given to their son, who became ill at football practice around 5:20 p.m. and was put on a school bus and returned to the high school shortly thereafter. Suspecting heat injury the boy was laid on the floor and covered with a blanket and unsuccessful attempts were made to give him salt water. His mother was called at 6:45 p.m. and she called a doctor who arrived at 7:15 p.m. The boy was immediately taken to a hospital for treatment, but his condition worsened and he died at 2:30 a.m. The cause of death was listed as heat stroke.

A doctor who treated the boy testified that covering the victim with a blanket was the improper thing to do and that time was of the essence in cases of heat stroke and quick treatment was necessary. The doctor said that had the boy received immediate and proper first aid, his death would have been much more unlikely.

The trial court dismissed the case without a written reason. The Court of Appeals reversed the dismissal, ruling that the two coaches who were present were negligent in denying the boy immediate medical assistance and in applying improper first aid. The court held that the evidence supported the premise that it was more likely than not that the boy would have survived with reasonable and prompt medical attention. The court ruled the evidence failed to support claims against the other defendants and held the two coaches and school board negligent. The court awarded each of the parents $20,000 plus medical and funeral costs.

Note. While the discussion here centered on the issue of improper first aid given to a heat stroke victim, another pertinent issue is raised for physical educators and coaches. Teachers and coaches who conduct activities in hot climates need to have clear guidelines for their practice or activity sessions which serve to reduce the risk of heat stroke occurring in the first place. The severity of a workout, the temperature, the number of rest breaks and the availability of water are all factors which need to be considered in planning for and conducting activity sessions in hot weather.

Welch v. Dunsmuir Joint Union High School District
326 P. 2d 633

Issue: First aid — Improperly moving injured student

Level of Court: Supreme Court, Appellate Division
Date/State: 1958/California
Decision: Plaintiff

The plaintiff was injured during a football scrimmage with another high school. After being hit while carrying the ball, the plaintiff fell forward and a tackler fell on top of him. After the hit and tackle, the plaintiff was unable to get to his feet. The coach suspected a neck injury. He had the plaintiff attempt to grip his hand, which he was able to do. Eight team members then moved the plaintiff off the playing field. A team doctor was present but did not come out onto the field. After arriving at the sideline, the plaintiff was no longer able to move either his hands or feet. He is now a permanent quadraplegic.

Expert testimony indicated that, given the existing circumstances, it was probable that additional spinal cord damage occurred after the initial injury as a result of improperly moving the plaintiff. The coach was found negligent by the court for not waiting for the doctor before moving the injured student and the doctor was found negligent for failing to act promptly. The court awarded $325,000 in damages.

The defendants appealed the lower court decision on a number of procedural grounds. The Supreme Court upheld the finding of negligence but amended the damages to $207,000.

Note: Even though this case is quite old it provides a sound warning to a continuing problem in sport. In the absence of trainers or doctors, coaches sometimes tend to be in too big a hurry to move injured players off to the sidelines of the playing field or court so that the game or contest can continue. Whenever suspecting neck or head injuries, coaches should proceed extremely cautiously as errors in judgment can have catastrophic consequences, as in this case. Whenever possible, professional help should be immediately sought and players moved only after they have been properly immobilized.

Wightman v. Town of Methuen
526 N.E. 2d 1079

Issue: Failure to seek immediate medical attention

Level of Court: Court of Appeals
Date/State: 1988/Massachusetts
Decision: Defendant/Affirmed

The plaintiff, a second grade student, was injured on the school playground before the start of school. An older boy picked him up by his legs and spun him around in the air. After repeatedly asking the older boy to stop, the plaintiff was thrown to the ground. The plaintiff went to two nearby staff members crying and in pain. The two staff members sent him on to class without examining his arm. The plaintiff's classroom teacher sent him to the nurse's office when it became obvious he was in pain and unable to participate in the class activities. No nurse was on duty. The physical education teacher applied first aid and the parents were called. The plaintiff had suffered multiple fractures of his right arm which required surgery. The plaintiff filed suit charging inadequate supervision and failure to seek immediate medical attention. The defendant moved for summary judgment claiming it was exempt from liability under the discretionary function exemption of the Massachussets Tort Claims Act. Summary judgment was granted for the defendant and the plaintiff appealed.

The Appellate Court upheld the lower court decision. It ruled that sizing up the gravity of a school yard fight, deciding how to deal with it, and maintaining school discipline involve "judgment, experience, and intuition which is the sum of experience" and required broad discretion. The court held that management of student fights and student discipline falls within the discretionary function exception of the Tort Claims Act and that the exception applies even where there has been abuse of discretion.

While noting that a failure to seek immediate medical attention does not fall within the discretionary function exemption to liability, the court ruled that this claim of the plaintiff failed because it was not properly presented. The Massachussets Tort Claims Act requires all claims be presented in writing to the executive officer of the public employer within two years of the incident giving rise to the claim before a civil action can be initiated. The plaintiff's letter to school officials made no mention of the failure to seek immediate medical attention. It addressed only the issue of supervision.

Note. Even if the required written notice of claim had been properly submitted, the plaintiff in this case would have had to show a causal connection between the school's failure to seek immediate medical attention and his ultimate injuries. The fractures were due to his fall. To collect any damages because of the school's negligence in not seeking immediate medical attention, evidence would have to show that the plaintiff's injuries were aggravated or made worse by the school's actions after the accident had occurred. No such evidence was submitted. It is important to note that it is not sufficient to merely show a negligent act occurred. To successfully collect damages in court, a plaintiff must show a causal connection between the alleged act and the ultimate injury.

Barth v. Board of Education of City of Chicago
490 N.E. 2d 77

Issue: Delay in medical treatment for head injury

Level of Court: Court of Appeals
Date/State: 1986/Illinois
Decision: Plaintiff/Affirmed

The plaintiff, then an 11-year-old sixth grader, received a head injury as a result of a collision with another boy during a morning recess kickball game supervised by the physical education teacher. After falling to the ground, both boys were assisted off the field by the physical educator. The plaintiff felt sick to his stomach and dizzy. A teacher aide escorted the boys to the principal's office where they arrived approximately five minutes after the accident. Both boys sat on a bench with the plaintiff still crying, holding his head and stomach. A red mark became noticeable on the side of the plaintiff's head where the blow occurred.

Five minutes after arriving in the office, the secretary called the homes of both boys to inform the parents of the accident. Unable to reach the plaintiff's mother at home, the secretary called her at work and left a message for her to call the school. The plaintiff's mother returned the call approximately 15 minutes later, by which time the plaintiff's color was bad and his eyes were glassy. Told that he had injured his head and appeared to be sick, the mother ordered the secretary to take the boy to the hospital and that she would arrive in approximately an hour from work and that the boy's brother would meet him at the hospital. The secretary then left an aide in charge while she went to find the assistant principal and inform her of the accident and her actions. The boy was now nauseous and had vomited three times. The secretary called 911, now 25 minutes after the accident, and requested an ambulance.

By the time the assistant principal returned to the office, the boy had lost color and was nodding his head up and down and complained of being tired. When the ambulance had not arrived 30 minutes later, 911 was called again. Being told the message was recorded and being handled, the school waited 15 more minutes and still no ambulance. A third call to 911 was made and the assistant principal requested to talk to the fire department directly. An ambulance was dispatched within a couple of minutes and arrived at the school two minutes later. The ambulance which took the boy had been parked at the hospital, which was directly across the street from the school. The boy arrived at the hospital an hour and a half after the accident. The boy was transferred to another hospital one hour and 20 minutes later and was operated on shortly after arrival to remove a blood clot from the brain.

The doctor testified he removed a hematoma the size of an orange from the top of the boy's head. He also testified the hour delay in transporting the boy to the hospital allowed the hematoma to "grow from the size of a walnut to the size of an orange." If the hematoma had been removed an hour earlier, the doctor testified the boy probably would have had a mere seven to ten day hospital stay. "Six years after the accident, the plaintiff's left side was still severely weak, he required a cane, his intellectual function was impaired, and he experienced severe headaches."

Under Illinois law, teachers and school districts are immune from liability for actions within the scope of their employment unless those actions constitute malfeasance or willful, wanton misconduct. The trial court found the district, the city, and its 911 operator guilty of willful and wanton misconduct. The Appellate Court upheld the trial court judgment and the plaintiff was awarded $2,550,000.

Note. The message presented by this case is clear. All head injuries should be considered serious unless shown to be otherwise. Where a serious head injury is suspected, prompt medical attention is absolutely essential. Any prolonged wait invites disastrous and sad consequences.

Gara v. Lomonaco
557 N.E. 2d 483

> Issue: Refusing to allow injured student to see nurse
> and improper matting for jazz dance

Level of Court: State Appellate Court
Date/State: 1990/Illinois
Decision: Defendant/Affirmed

The plaintiff was injured in her physical education class while participating in jazz dance which was being conducted on the wrestling mats. The mats being used were not taped down and overlapped. While performing, the plaintiff caught her foot between two of the mats and fell, injuring her ankle. The physical education teacher did not examine the ankle and allegedly refused to allow the plaintiff to be excused to see the nurse. During her next two class periods the plaintiff again sought permission to see the nurse but was denied permission to see the nurse by her teachers. It was later discovered that the plaintiff had a fractured ankle.

The district filed a motion for dismissal, alleging that the complaint failed to state a proper cause for action. The district's request was based on their claim of governmental immunity under Illinois statute. The trial court granted the district's motion and the plaintiff appealed.

The Appellate Court upheld the lower court ruling while holding that the teacher's decision to not allow the plaintiff to see the nurse fell within her supervisory duty and was, therefore, immune to suit unless it could be shown that her actions constituted willful and wanton conduct. After reviewing the complaint, the court did not view the refusal to see the nurse as willful and wanton conduct. The court also held that the plaintiff failed to adequately plead how the use of untaped and overlapping wrestling mats for the dance activity constituted willful and wanton conduct.

Note. This case serves as a useful reminder to physical educators and coaches to give careful consideration to the playing surface on which they conduct their activities. More importantly, the need to not second guess student complaints of injury or illness should be strongly emphasized. Physical educators and coaches are trained to provide first aid where appropriate, but *are not* in a position to diagnose injuries or illness.

Without the protection of governmental immunity, the outcome of this case could have been different if the failure to seek medical attention had aggravated the initial injury. Even with governmental immunity, a better worded complaint might have adequately presented a case for willful and wanton conduct in the securing of treatment for the injured student.

Peck v. The Board of Education of the
City of Mount Vernon
283 N.E. 2d 618

Issue: Immediacy of first aid

Level of Court: State Court of Appeals
Date/State: 1972/New York
Decision: Plaintiff/Defendant/Defendant

The plaintiff's son died as a result of accidently being kicked in the head during his physical education class. Suffering from headache and dizziness, the boy was checked by the school nurse. He had not lost consciousness and the nurse found no pupillary changes. Within 50 minutes of the accident, the boy and a friend left school to see the boy's physician. The physician sent him to the hospital where he was admitted two hours after the accident. X-rays did not disclose the skull fracture and blood clot which ultimately took the boy's life.

The neurosurgeon who treated the boy testified that an earlier operation could have saved the boy's life but was not certain as to how much sooner would have been necessary. He also testified that headache and dizziness were both "soft" symptoms of brain injury and that the boy did not display any critical signs of severe head trauma.

The trial court finding for the plaintiff was reversed by the Supreme Court, Appellate Division. The Court of Appeals upheld the reversal while ruling the evidence failed to prove any unreasonable delay of medical attention by the school district.

Note. All head injuries should be taken seriously. Where head injuries occur, parents should always be notified. When dealing with head injuries, failure to error on the side of caution can often result in tragic consequences. Teachers and coaches should consider the mechanism of injury as well as symptoms when picking a course of action relative to first aid for head injuries. Prudence dictates observation and notification of parents at a minimum.

O'Brien v. Township High School District 214
415 N.E. 2d 1015

Issue: First aid delegated to another student

Level of Court: State Appellate Court
Date/State: 1980/Illinois
Decision: Defendant/Affirmed in part and reversed in part/
                Reversed and remanded

The plaintiff brought suit against the school district, two teachers, as well as a fellow student. The plaintiff had a pre-existing condition of septicemia in his left knee. The injury, which was received off school property in an activity unrelated to school, was treated by another student at the direction of the plaintiff's teacher. The plaintiff alleged that the "medical and surgical" treatment of the injured knee by the student was given negligently and without parental consent and resulted in severe and permanent injury. The plaintiff also alleged that the defendants were willful and wanton in their conduct.

The trial court dismissed the case against all defendants based on their claim to immunity. On appeal, the Court of Appeals held that teachers act in loco parentis and are generally only liable for willful and wanton acts. The court concluded that their actions did not rise to the willful and wanton standard. The court ruled, however, that the district was not protected by governmental immunity in this case. The court stated that school districts are liable for willful and wanton misconduct when it involves an injury which arises out of the personal supervision and control of a student by a teacher or the maintenance of a "sound learning atmosphere." The court concluded that the broad discretion granted in the areas of supervision and discipline is not required in situations where medical treatment is provided. The court ruled that public policy dictated that any such treatment be competently rendered. The court upheld the dismissal of willful and wanton misconduct charges against the teachers but reversed the dismissal of the negligence charges against the school district.

The school district appealed to the Supreme Court which concluded that the school code and immunity statute did not provide immunity to the district and its employees under the circumstances presented by this case. While recognizing that districts and their employees stand in loco parentis relative to their supervision, discipline and conduct of the school program, the court held that teachers are not privileged to do everything that a parent may do. The court ruled that the seeking of medical treatment for the plaintiff was the responsibility of the parents and outside of the supervisory responsibility of the teachers. The court held that the teachers in this case could be held liable for negligently "prescribing or administering treatment which causes injury." The Supreme Court upheld the court of appeals ruling on the issue of ordinary negligence on the part of the school district and reversed the dismissal of the willful and wanton misconduct complaint against the teachers. The judgment of the trial court was therefore reversed in its entirety and the case remanded to the trial court for trial on its merits.

IN SUMMARY

THE REASONABLY PRUDENT PHYSICAL
EDUCATOR OR COACH:

1. Is familiar with injuries which are common to the activities being taught and is knowledgeable about the first aid required for these injuries.

2. Does not diagnose or treat head injuries.

3. Considers all head injuries serious and follows established procedures for first aid, notification of parents, and the securing of medical attention.

4. Has an adequately equipped first aid kit available at all activity, practice, and game sessions.

5. Keeps an accurate record of all accidents and actions taken as well as a file of all medical information provided by parents or doctors.

6. Requires a doctor's note giving permission to resume activity following any serious illness or injury for which a doctor has excused a student or athlete from activity.

7. Seeks immediate medical attention whenever the circumstances warrant it.

8. Has a medical treatment authorization card in their possession whenever traveling out of town for games.

9. Has an emergency contact and information card for each athlete in their possession at all practices and games.

10. Together with the administration, develops a building plan for dealing with serious injuries.

TRANSPORTATION

While transportation is not, in most cases, a formal duty of physical educators or coaches, it is often one they voluntarily assume as they transport students to and from special events and extracurricular activities. This practice raises a number of issues and concerns.

The transportation of students to and from special events and extracurricular activities can be accomplished in one of four ways. They may be transported by independent contractor, by school vehicles driven by licensed district employees, by an employee's vehicle, or by private vehicles driven by volunteers. The potential for liability varies from situation to situation with the least potential for liability existing where independent contractors are used and the greatest potential where private vehicles operated by volunteers are employed.

When an independent contractor is employed by a district to transport students, the district, for the most part, transfers its liability to the independent contractor. A duty of care still exists, however, relative to the selection and retention of the contractor. Issues such as the licensing and certification of drivers, liability insurance, and the past record of the selected company need to be considered.

Transportation of students by district vehicle is usually accomplished by either school bus or passenger vans. Buses are the best maintained vehicles in the district fleet. They make daily trips in and out of the bus garage and the daily availability of servicing staff to attend to maintenance needs is present. They are also operated by trained personnel.

Vans, on the other hand, are the least maintained vehicles in the fleet. Because they are typically housed at school sites and are driven by teachers and coaches, district motor pool staff must often rely on the teacher or coach to alert them to servicing and repair needs. The driver of any district vehicle has the duty to promptly report any necessary maintenance or repair needs.

Any vehicle with a potentially hazardous condition such as broken mirrors, burnt-out lights/flasher bulbs, doors which cannot be opened, tires low on tread, or broken seat belts should not be used until the hazardous condition has been corrected. It is not enough to simply report the condition. Report and then do not use the vehicle until it is attended to. Each vehicle should be supplied with all necessary emergency equipment such as flares, markers, first aid kit, and traction devices during increment weather. Care also needs to be taken to not overload vehicles.

The Eugene School District in Eugene, Oregon, has taken strong measures to promote safety in the transportation of students by district vehicles (12 and 20 passenger vans) which are operated by teachers and coaches. Anyone who transports students with district vehicles must be certified. The certification process includes obtaining current first aid and CPR certification as well as attending a two-hour class at the transportation department. The class covers characteristics of the vehicle, operation of the vehicle, emergency procedures, and driver expectations relative to reporting and obtaining necessary servicing and repair. The class also details requirements of drivers relative to the use of alcohol and the allowed maximum amount of daily on-duty time including driving. Driving records are checked with the Oregon Department of Motor Vehicles and the district has a network which allows it to be notified of changes in that record due to either moving citations or accidents. A point deduction system has been developed for citations and accidents which allows for objective decisions relative to certification and the maintenance of certification for drivers. The Eugene model is an excellent one for those districts which choose to allow their teaching and coaching staff to transport students with district vehicles.

The use of employee cars increases the potential for driver liability significantly. The owner of the car has responsibility for the maintenance of the vehicle and any lack of maintenance which is connected to an injury accident could leave the employee liable. Employees who drive students or athletes should have adequate insurance coverage, especially in the area of PIP (personal injury protection). The owner/driver also needs to be aware of any limitations on their coverage. A number of PIP policies become void if the driver accepts any compensation for the use of his/her vehicle.

Compensation can also impact liability in those jurisdictions which have guest statutes on the books. Guest statutes provide liability only for willful and wanton misconduct when the injured party rode as a guest of the driver. If the purpose of a trip is primarily for business, rather than pleasure, and there is any direct or indirect compensation of the owner or operator of the vehicle, the guest relationship does not exist. Where the guest relationship does not exist, the driver is liable for ordinary negligence. Where transportation is being provided for team members to games, they generally fall outside of the guest relationship.

The casual use of private vehicles operated by volunteers is a risky practice for schools, teachers or coaches to employ when transporting students or athletes. There is generally no knowledge of the driving record of these volunteers nor knowledge of the maintenance history of the vehicles being used. The teacher or coach in these cases is usually "contracting blind" with a parent or volunteer for the transportation. The same issues relative to PIP coverage, guest statutes, and reimbursement previously discussed apply here as well. If the decision is made to use private vehicles operated by parents or volunteers, the employee in charge of the activity needs to be aware of the insurance coverage of the driver, the condition of the vehicle, and the reliability of the driver as well as his/her driving record. The employee should ensure that no vehicle is overloaded and that each student or athlete has both a seat and seat belt. As with all vehicles, the car of the parent or volunteer should be provided with emergency equipment such as flares, markers, and first aid supplies.

The amount of case law relevant to the transportation of students and athletes by teachers and coaches in the K-12 school setting is limited. This is due in large part to the statutory requirements of insurance coverage which usually allows claims to be settled outside of litigation.

The following cases offer some illustration of the points which have been discussed.

Brown v. Egan Consolidated School District 50-2
449 N.W. 2d 259

Issue: Lack of emergency lights or warning devices

Level of court: State Supreme Court
Date/State: 1989/South Dakota
Decision: Plaintiff/Affirmed

The plaintiff collided with a school bus while driving to work. Evidence at the trial court indicated the weather on the date of the accident was blizzard-like with blowing snow, poor visibility, and icy roads. The plaintiff came across the bus which was stopped in the middle of the road without any emergency lights, brake lights, tail lights, or any other warning devices. The plaintiff was unable to stop her car and rear-ended the bus. She suffered a severed aorta, broken leg, broken hip, and other serious injuries.

The school district filed for summary judgment based on its claim of governmental immunity. The trial court denied the district's motion and the district appealed. On appeal, the Supreme Court upheld the lower court decision. The court ruled that a South Dakota statute waiving liability for use of a school bus by outside nonprofit organizations did not apply to school districts transporting their own students to and from school or for interscholastic activities. The court held that the district had waived its immunity up to the limits of its insurance coverage which, in this case, was $400,000.

McKee v. Southeast Delco School District
512 A. 2d 28

Issue: Use of seat belts in school vans

Level of Court: Superior Court
Date/State: 1986/Pennsylvania
Decision: Defendant/Set aside for new trial/Affirmed

The plaintiff, a six-year-old elementary school student, received mouth and jaw injuries as a result of being thrown forward from her seat into the console of the van in which she was riding as it braked to avoid colliding with another car. The van was owned and operated by a private company. The jury returned a verdict in favor of the defendants. The trial court set aside the jury verdict and ordered a new trial because it determined it had improperly excluded evidence regarding the failure of the driver to use available seat belts to restrain the plaintiff. The defendants appealed the order for a new trial.

On appeal, the Superior Court noted that the admissibility of evidence regarding the non-use of seat belts has usually been dealt with in cases where their non-use has attempted to show contributory negligence on the part of plaintiffs. These courts have generally held that absent a statutory mandate, a person has no duty to wear a seat belt and that the admissibility of evidence regarding their use was not allowed in attempting to establish contributory negligence. Other courts have held that depending upon the circumstances, failure to wear a seat belt could constitute contributory negligence. The Superior Court stated that these courts have at least implicitly held that there is a duty to use seat belts even in the absence of a statutory mandate.

The Superior Court held that the facts in this case could lead a jury to find that the driver of the van had a duty to restrain the children in the van by using the seat belts. It took note that the plaintiffs were prepared to show that the district had instructed the owner of the van to restrain the children with seat belts and that the owner of the van had given its drivers instructions that seat belts were to be worn. The Superior Court affirmed the lower court order for a new trial.

Adams v. Kline
239 A. 2d 230

Issue: Overloading vehicle

Level of Court: Superior Court
Date/State: 1968/Delaware
Decision: Plaintiff

The plaintiff was injured in an automobile accident while transporting other team members and equipment to an away game. Evidence indicated that two vehicles were used to transport the university soccer team to its game. The lead vehicle was driven by the coach while the other vehicle, a university owned van, was driven by the plaintiff. The van which the plaintiff was driving carried six other players as well as all the team gear. The lead vehicle braked suddenly for a yellow light and the van driven by the plaintiff was unable to stop as it struck the lead vehicle in the rear.

The plaintiff filed suit claiming negligence on a number of grounds. He alleged that the coach:

1. Failed to inspect and, therefore, discover the allegedly defective brakes;

2. Allowed the van to be overloaded;
3. Failed to determine whether he was a competent driver;
4. Failed to instruct the plaintiff in the correct operation of the van;
5. Failed to determine if the plaintiff had a valid driver's and chauffeur's license;
6. Failed to determine whether he met the 21 year age requirement for driving a school bus.

The defendant claimed the plaintiff was contributorily negligent and moved for a summary judgment on all allegations. The motion was denied.

Evidence indicated that the plaintiff was a competent driver who had experience driving heavy duty equipment of all types. It further indicated that when traveling to away games, the drivers of the vehicles were simply determined by who got behind the wheel. The van had a carrying capacity of 900 pounds and was alleged to be carrying 1300 to1400 pounds on the day of the accident.

The court ruled that the evidence failed to support any allegation of defective brakes and held the coach did not have any duty to personally inspect the brakes. The court also held that the evidence did not sufficiently support the allegations regarding the coach's and university's failure to determine the competence of the driver and the licenses he possessed or their failure to instruct him in the operation of the van, as none of these could be found to be the proximate cause of the injury.

Summary judgment was granted to the defendants on these allegations. However, the court ruled against the defendants as to their motion for summary judgment related to the allegation of overloading the vehicle. The court held that if it could be shown that the coach allowed the vehicle to be overloaded and that the overloading of the vehicle could be foreseen to affect the ability of the van to stop in a safe distance, a jury might find negligence. Summary judgment on this allegation was denied.

Hoover v. Charlotte - Mecklenburg Board of Education
361 S.E. 2d 93

Issue: Inspection and maintenance of school bus

Level of Court: Court of Appeals
Date/State: 1987/North Carolina
Decision: Defendant/Affirmed

The plaintiff was injured when the rear wheel assembly disengaged from the chassis of the school bus in which she was riding, causing the bus to crash. The North Carolina Industrial Commission cleared the bus driver as well as the district and its maintenance department of all charges of negligence. Their decision was appealed to the state Court of Appeals.

The Court of Appeals affirmed the decision for the defendants. The court ruled that the evidence submitted before the commission supported its findings that:

1. The school bus driver drove the vehicle in a proper manner and had no warning or indication that the rear wheel assembly was going to come off the bus until it actually occurred.
2. The maintenance department had acted reasonably and prudently in that regular monthly inspections were completed on the bus as well as detailed annual inspections. The last inspection did not indicate any problem with the assembly.

The plaintiff contended that the commission erred in not finding the district negligent under the doctrine of res ipsa loquitas. This doctrine states that "the thing speaks for itself" and that under the circumstances, the accident is one which would not have occurred but for negligence. The court ruled that there was no reason to believe that the commission did not consider all of the evidence, res ipsa loquitas included, in making its findings and conclusions of no negligence in the maintenance, repair, or operation of the school bus.

Blair v. Board of Education of
Sherburne - Earlville Central School
448 N.Y.S. 2d 566

Issue: Supervision on bus

Level of Court: Supreme Court, Appellate Division
Date/State: 1982/New York
Decision: Plaintiff/Affirmed

The plaintiff suffered a serious permanent eye injury when struck by an object thrown by another student while riding the school bus. The plaintiff alleged negligence in supervision. Evidence indicated that horseplay and the throwing of objects had gone on for 15 minutes prior to the accident and that the driver took no action to stop it. Testimony indicated the driver was even alerted to the dangerous situation by one of the student passengers. The trial court found for the plaintiff and awarded $102,600 in damages. The Supreme Court upheld the lower court decision while holding the driver responsible for controlling student behavior.

Note. This accident occurred while transporting students home from school. The bus driver, being the only adult aboard the bus, had the dual responsibility of driving and supervising students. This is a standard practice in the transportation of students to and from school.

Transportation of athletes to another school for competition presents a different situation. In this case, the bus driver is joined by one or more coaches. It would be unwise for coaches to assume that the bus driver, in this situation, has the sole responsibility of supervising students. The supervisory duty of bus drivers in this situation clearly becomes secondary to the duty owed by the coach. Clear expectations for the bus driver and the coach should be developed and clearly communicated to all members of the transportation and athletic departments.

Lofy v. Joint School District #2, City of Cumberland
166 N.W. 2d 809

Issue: Transfer of liability to independent contractor

Level of Court: Supreme Court
Date/State: 1969/Wisconsin
Decision: Defendant/Affirmed

The plaintiff was injured, and her husband killed, as a result of a multi-vehicle accident in which a bus, chartered by the school district to transport students to a basketball tournament, rear-ended their car. The school district moved for summary judgment claiming it was not liable for any negligence on the part of the transportation company with which it contracted. The trial court granted the district's motion and the plaintiff appealed.

On appeal, the Supreme Court upheld the lower court decision. The court ruled that one who contracts with an independent contractor is generally not liable for the acts of the independent contractor. While noting that a district may not delegate its liability where the services contracted for involve inherent danger, the court held the transportation of students by bus between two cities could not be held to be inherently dangerous.

IN SUMMARY

THE REASONABLY PRUDENT PHYSICAL EDUCATOR OR COACH:

1. Refrains from using anything other than district vehicles to transport students and athletes.

2. Never overloads a vehicle.

3. Makes sure each rider has a designated seat and uses a seat belt if one is provided.

4. Completes a visual check of a vehicle as well as a check of all lights, blinkers, tires, and wipers whenever a vehicle other than a school bus is used. Does not use any vehicle which is not well maintained.

5. Immediately reports any maintenance or safety needs of any district vehicle which he/she uses to transport students.

6. Makes sure any vehicle used is equipped and supplied with adequate warning devices such as markers and flairs.

7. Equips any vehicle used to transport students or athletes with a first aid kit.

8. Never arranges for students or athletes to drive.

9. Provides adequate supervision within the vehicle.

10. Makes sure any vehicle used is properly insured and that all drivers are properly licensed. In a number of states, a large passenger van full of riders requires the driver to have a chauffeur's license.

MISCELLANEOUS ISSUES

PERMISSION SLIPS, WAIVERS, AND RELEASES

In conjuction with the many special events and outings in which physical educators and coaches involve their students, both parents and students are often asked to sign permission slips, waivers, and releases. The same requirement is also sometimes a prerequisite to participation by students in interscholastic athletic programs. While each of these forms serve a sound administrative function, it is important that physical educators and coaches understand that they do little and, in most cases, nothing to relieve them of liability for their negligent acts.

Permission slips are exactly that, permission slips. They inform the parent of the particulars of a given activity and solicit their permission for their child to participate. The mere granting of permission to participate is not a waiver or a release. While they serve the useful function of providing information and public relations, they do nothing to relieve liability for negligent acts.

Waivers and releases attempt to waive the rights of parents and students to sue school districts and their employees for their negligent acts. They amount to a contract to not hold a party liable for their future negligent acts. As such, they represent an expressed assumption of risk. As was discussed in the section of the assumption of risk doctrine, the concept, when used as a defense against a negligence claim, requires the actual knowledge and understanding of the risks assumed and the voluntary assumption of those risks. If either of these factors is missing, the assumption of risk defense fails. Waivers and releases should provide clear warnings relative to the hazards and risks associated with participation in the particular activity being entered into. They should specifically detail the risks to be assumed and should also include the responsibilities of the individual engaging in the activity covered by the agreement.

While the law has long recognized the right of individuals to contract with others to limit liability, they have been equally strong in holding such agreements invalid where they are contrary to public policy. They have also recognized that minors may not legally enter into contracts or have their rights waived by their parents. As a result, parents may sign away their own right to sue through a waiver or release provided the agreement is both clear as to what is being waived and is not contrary to public policy. They may not, however, sign away the rights of their injured child to sue.

Waivers and releases which have attempted to waive the liability of schools and their employees for school activities have usually been held to be contrary to public policy. However, while generally invalid as a complete waiver of the right to sue, a well written waiver, release, or agreement to participate can be very useful in defending a teacher, coach, or school district against a negligence claim. The information contained within these documents can often be used to help substantiate defense claims of contributory negligence, implied assumption of risk or comparative negligence on the part of an injured plaintiff. They can be effectively used to demonstrate plaintiff knowledge of both the risks involved in and the responsibilities required for participation in a given activity.

Indemnity agreements differ slightly from waivers and releases. Where waivers and releases attempt to waive liability for negligent acts, indemnity agreements attempt to shift the financial burden for injuries arising out of negligent acts from one party to another. The right to sue is maintained but the parent, in this case, would be relieving the school or employee of the burden of paying financial damages. Like waivers and releases, indemnity agreements can be entered into by adults only and parents may not waive the right of their children to recover damages in their own right. Indemnity agreements which have attempted to hold school districts and their employees harmless for their negligent acts have generally been held to be contrary to public policy.

The following case from the state of Washington outlines a six-part test employed by courts when determining whether waivers and releases are contrary to public policy and, thereby, invalid.

Wagenblast v. Odessa School District
758 P. 2d 968

Issue: Waivers and releases

Level of Court: State Supreme Court
Date/State: 1988/Washington
Decision: Plaintiff/Affirmed

Suit was filed on behalf of four Odessa School District students who, along with their parents, were required to sign liability releases (exculpatory agreements) as a condition to their participation in interscholastic athletics. The releases attempted to waive district liability for any ordinary negligence which might arise in connection with the district's interscholastic athletic program. The trial court granted summary judgment for the plaintiff and permanently restrained the Odessa School District from requiring the students and their parents to sign the releases. The school district appealed the decision directly to the State Supreme Court. The State Supreme Court consolidated this appeal with an appeal of a Seattle case which had been filed with the State Court of Appeals. In the Seattle case, the Superior Court of King County denied the request for injunctive and declaratory relief against the use of waivers and releases as a condition for participation in an athletic program.

The Supreme Court upheld the decision against the Odessa School District and reversed the Seattle decision. The court held that the releases which public school students were required to sign as a condition of engaging in school-related activities and which released school districts from consequences of all future school district negligence were invalid in that they were a violation of public policy. The court noted that while parties may contract with one another to not hold each other liable, there are instances where public policy reasons for preserving the duty of care owed by one to another outweighs the freedom to contract. Relying on a decision of the California Supreme Court in Tunkl v. Regents of University of California, 383 P. 2d 441 (1963), the court applied the test used in Tunkl to the cases at hand. The Tunkl decision outlined six characteristics of exculpatory agreements which need to be considered when determining the validity of any agreement. The Washington Supreme Court noted that the more of the six characteristics that appear in an agreement, the more likely it would be declared invalid on public policy grounds. It held that all six characteristics were present in the current cases. The six characteristics examined in deciding this case were as follows:

1. "The agreement concerns an endeavor of a type generally thought suitable for public regulation." Interscholastic sports are clearly regulated to an extensive degree by local school boards as well as the state activities association.

2. "The party seeking exculpation is engaged in performing a service of great importance to the public, which is often a matter of practical necessity for some members of the public." While students have no fundamental right to participate in interscholastic sports, it is nonetheless considered an integral and important part of the total educational program by both students and the general public.

3. "Such party holds itself out as willing to perform this service for any member of the public who seeks it, or at least for any member coming within certain established standards." Interscholastic sports are clearly open to all students who meet certain skill and eligibility requirements.

4. "Because of the essential nature of the service, in the economic setting of the transaction, the party invoking the exculpation possesses a decisive advantage of bargaining strength against any member of the public who seeks the services." In most instances, alternative programs of organized competition do not exist. Where outside alternatives exist for some activities, they lack the attraction of interscholastic competition and often have a high cost associated with them. Because of the high importance of interscholastic sports and limited alternatives to its activities, schools

are viewed to have a near monopoly and, therefore, clearly enjoy disparate bargaining strength
when they require the signing of releases.

5. "In exercising a superior bargaining power the
party confronts the public with a standardized
adhesion contract of exculpation, and makes no
provision whereby a purchaser may pay additional reasonable fees and obtain protection
against negligence." In both cases before this
court, the policies regarding releases are
unwaivering. Students and parents have no
alternative but to sign or be barred from participation.

6. "The person or property of members of the public
seeking such services must be placed under the
control of the furnisher of services, subject to the
risk of carelessness on the part of the furnisher,
its employees or agents." The court noted that
school districts owe a duty to students to use
ordinary care and to anticipate reasonably
foreseeable dangers and to take reasonable
precautions to protect students from those
dangers. Due to the coach-athlete relationship,
the student athlete is placed under the control of
the coach. By signing the release, the student
athlete becomes subject to the risk that the school
district will breach their required duty of care.

IN SUMMARY

THE REASONABLY PRUDENT PHYSICAL EDUCATOR OR COACH:

1. Makes use of permission forms where appropriate to properly notify parents of the particulars of an activity and to seek their permission.

2. Does not rely on waivers or releases for absolute protection from liability.

3. Uses "agreement to participate" documents which give clear and appropriate warnings of specific injuries and all known risks associated with participation in a given activity. These documents should also include behavior, training and performance expectations for participants.

TANGENT PROGRAMS AND SCOPE OF EMPLOYMENT

Club Activities, Summer Camps, Summer Leagues, Enrichment Activities

Scope of employment can have major implications for the personal liability of teachers and coaches. Scope of employment is defined to include those acts of an employee which are done "in the furtherance of duties he owes to his employer and where the employer is, or could be, exercising some control, either directly or indirectly over the employee's activities."[17] Physical educators often find themselves in a grey area where the question of scope of employment is not clear cut. They often engage their students and athletes in activities which are related in purpose to their school programs yet not officially sponsored by the school or district. These activities usually occur either after school hours or during vacation periods. They include, but are not limited to, club activities, summer team camps, summer leagues, and enrichment activities. The following case and discussion is presented to help clarify the scope of employment issue and the concerns which need to be addressed by physical education and athletic personnel who engage in these activities which are tangent to the regular school program.

Rollins v. Blair
767 P. 2d 328

Issue: Liability for cheerleader injury during summer clinic

Level of Court: Supreme Court
Date/State: 1989/Montana
Decision: Defendant/Affirmed

The plaintiff, a high school varsity cheerleader, injured her lower back in a fall from a pyramid being practiced by her cheerleading squad. At the time of the accident, the plaintiff and the rest of the school's cheerleading squad were attending a cheerleading camp which was being run by a private entity at Montana State University. The plaintiff brought suit against the camp sponsor, the National Cheerleaders Association, the high school, and the school district alleging negligent supervision. The trial court awarded summary judgment for both the high school and school district and the jury returned a verdict in favor of the program sponsor and the National Cheerleaders Association.

Testimony at the trial court indicated the injury occurred during a free period before evening activities when the girls were practicing the "home cheer." The pyramid being practiced by the girls was one which they had practiced for over two months before coming to the camp and one which they had performed during past athletic contests. The plaintiff was aware that injury could occur from participating in pyramids as she had injured her ankle and another cheerleader had broken her ankle from previous falls prior to the camp. Testimony also showed that the cheerleader advisor for the plaintiff's high school attended the clinic and that transportation to the clinic was by a bus provided by the school. The funds to attend the clinic were raised by the girls themselves and deposited in school district accounts. Camp employees testified that a meeting was held at the beginning of the camp for all the advisors which warned them about safety precautions, such as spotting. The head instructor testified that the camp neither taught nor encouraged the practice of the pyramid. Evidence showed the plaintiff's advisor did not attend the advisor's meeting, was not present at the time of the accident, and was not experienced in cheerleading.

The Supreme Court upheld the trial court decision for the defendants. The court held that the high school and school district were in no way involved with the camp with the exception of providing a bus for transportation. The court held that the high school was not liable for any negligence on the part of the squad advisor. This holding was based on the fact that she was not under contract with the school district during summer months, she used her own funds to attend the camp, and her attendance was personal and not as an employee of the school. They held that the advisor in this situation was not an agent of the district and, therefore, the district owed no duty to the plaintiff under the doctrine of respondeat superior. The court further ruled that there was no reversible error on the part of the district court which would allow a reversal of the jury verdict in favor of the camp sponsor.

Note: Physical educators and coaches often find themselves involved in activities outside the immediate scope of the school program. These activities, such as team camps and summer club activities and competition, are usually intended to give students and athletes additional opportunities to develop their skills. They are clearly used to help further develop school programs. It is important that teachers and coaches who become involved in these programs take steps to protect themselves in case of litigation.

In a good number of states where immunity has been abrogated by tort claims acts, teachers and coaches are protected from financial liability by hold-harmless statutes. A hold-harmless statute requires a school district to indemnify its employees against liability for their actions which occur within the scope of their employment. For those actions which fall outside the scope of their employment, teachers and coaches are personally liable. If a teacher or coach is going to involve him/herself and student athletes in tangent activities such as team camps, summer leagues, or club competition, it is a good idea to involve the school and administration to the greatest degree possible. Use of school facilities, school equipment, school uniforms, school or student body funds, and the knowledge of and any exercise of control over the activities by the administration, will all be factors considered in determining whether the activity falls within the full scope of employment. Scope of employment is not merely a function of regular work hours or contract year.

In the case discussed here, the cheerleader advisor was found to be acting outside the scope of her employment. Not only did the activity occur during the summer vacation months, but the involvement of the school district was nonexistent with the exception of providing bus transportation. If the district is not sufficiently entangled in the activity and any question exists as to whether a tangent activity falls outside the scope of employment, teachers and coaches involved in such activities would be wise to protect themselves with personal liability insurance.

IN SUMMARY

THE REASONABLY PRUDENT PHYSICAL
EDUCATOR OR COACH:

1. Secures personal liability insurance to provide protection for all tangent activities which might fall outside "the scope of employment."

2. Informs and *involves* the school administration and the school district to the greatest extent possible in all tangent activities in which he/she involves students or athletes.

PRACTICUM STUDENTS AND STUDENT TEACHERS

The use of practicum students and student teachers is commonplace in a good number of elementary and secondary school programs. While field-based experience programs fulfill an important state objective in training prospective teachers, a number of issues and concerns relative to liability arise due to the inexperience which these individuals bring to the school program.

Practicum students and student teachers are held to the same standard as an experienced teacher. They are expected to act in the manner of a reasonably prudent person who is qualified and trained to carry out the responsibilities of teaching and/or coaching. In the event of an injury, their actions will be gauged against the accepted standards employed in the field and endorsed by professional organizations and literature. Their actions will not be discounted in any way due to their lack of experience. The same is true for teacher aides who are left in charge of classes.

The question becomes, who is liable for injuries which occur in a practicum or student teaching situation? As with anyone, practicum students and student teachers are liable for their own acts and omissions. Can the cooperating teacher, supervising teacher, school district, and university be liable for injuries which occur to students or athletes under the control of the practicum student or student teacher? The answer is clearly, yes!

The individual financial liability of the practicum student or student teacher can vary from jurisdiction to jurisdiction. Sometimes, these students are paid a nominal salary which enables them to be clearly identified as a district employee and thereby covered by the insurance afforded to all other employees. They are often asked by their universities to purchase liability insurance to protect them during the course of their assignment. Many states have enacted statutes which grant student teachers and practicum students the status of an agent of the school which thereby extends the same liability protection to them as is extended to regular certified teachers. This status conferred by statute also extends hold-harmless or indemnification protection in many of the states where such legislation protects regular employees.

State statute and supporting administrative rules may, in many circumstances, dictate the duties and responsibilities which a practicum student or student teacher may or may not assume. It is important that any cooperating teacher fully understand his/her state statutes as they relate to student teachers. It is also imperative that the cooperating teacher fully understands the rules and guidelines for the practicum or student teaching experience. These are included in the contract between the sponsoring university and the cooperating school district.

Student teachers stand in the same relationship to their supervising and cooperating teacher as any other employee to his/her immediate supervisor. This relationship and the doctrine of respondeat superior dictates a number of responsibilities, duties, and concerns for the cooperating teacher and his or her school district. Of particular importance is an assessment of the practicum student or student teacher's abilities as well as areas of weakness. This can be accomplished through a review of their transcript as well as a conference with the university supervising teacher. This should be done prior to commencing the practicum or student teaching experience. The administration as well as the cooperating teacher should ensure that the prospective practicum student or student teacher is provided adequate orientation to the teaching and school situation to which he/she is assigned. Most critical, the cooperating teacher needs to provide active, ongoing supervision. While the practicum student or student teacher can be held personally liable, the cooperating teacher still retains legal control and responsibility for the class which has been assigned to him or her. That responsibility cannot be delegated away. The supervision and control exerted over the student teacher and the classroom must meet the reasonable and prudent standards as dictated by accepted professional practice and by guidelines set forth in the contract between the school district and the sponsoring university.

While the amount of litigation in this area has been minor, the need for concern is very real in a time when litigation continues to increase significantly. Most case law involving student teachers is rather old and occurred prior to legislation which has, in many cases, helped define both the role and status of practicum students and student teachers.

Three relatively recent cases are presented here.

Yarborough v. City University of New York
520 N.Y.S 2d 518

Issue: Equipment dangerous for its intended use
supplied by student teacher

Level of Court: Court of Claims
Date/State: 1987/New York
Decision: Plaintiff

The plaintiff, an elementary education major enrolled in a physical education methods course, received injuries as a result of her participation in class. Testimony indicated that on the day of the accident, instruction was being given by one of the students under the supervision of the professor in charge of the class. The class session for this day focused on relays. The plaintiff was injured while participating in a sack race on the gym floor. The plaintiff fell as she made her turn for the finish. The student assigned to prepare the activity explained how the race was to be run, demonstrated how it was to be run by hopping with both feet in the bag, divided the class into two teams, and provided each team with a plastic garbage bag. No instruction was given relative to the positioning of student's feet within the bag.

The Court of Claims held that a teacher is under a duty to use reasonable care to prevent injury to students and that this duty included not directing students to do something which is unreasonably dangerous and to ensure that equipment which is supplied to students is reasonably safe for its intended use. It also held that the duty included providing reasonable instruction and supervision which would allow students to safely perform the assigned tasks or use the supplied equipment. The court ruled that the defendant breached this duty by allowing or requiring students to perform the relay race on a wooden floor using a plastic bag. The court agreed with the expert testimony that indicated this created a foreseeable risk of injury. The court held that the risk of injury was further enhanced by the instructor's failure to instruct the plaintiff on the proper technique for performing the task, specifically, keeping the feet together. The court found the defendant 75 percent negligent while holding the plaintiff 25 percent contributorily negligent.

Mercantel v. Allen Parish School Board
490 So. 2d 1162

Issue: Improper supervision — Teacher aide left in
charge of class

Level of Court: State Court of Appeals
Date/State: 1986/Louisiana
Decision: Plaintiff/Modified and affirmed

The plaintiff, a 12-year-old seventh grader, fractured his femur during his physical education class while playing a makeshift football game using a paper cup. Evidence at the trial court indicated the physical education teacher was called to the principal's office for a conference and a teacher aide was sent to cover the class. During the teacher's absence, the makeshift game, which included tackling, got underway. The accident occurred toward the end of the period and testimony was conflicting as to whether or not the teacher had returned to the class prior to the injury occurring.

The game had lasted somewhere between 10-20 minutes. As a result of the accident, the plaintiff spent five and a half weeks in the hospital in traction, and was then placed in a cast from the chest down for an additional five to six weeks at home. Once out of the cast, he was confined to a wheelchair for another month and a walker for two months after that. As a result of the injury, the plaintiff suffered a premature closure of the growth plate in his right leg, which was then two and a half inches shorter than his left.

The trial court found the district negligent for failing to properly supervise the class but absolved both the teacher and the teacher aide of all liability. The trial court awarded $200,000 for the plaintiff. The decision was appealed by both the plaintiff and the defendant.

On appeal, the Appellate Court stated the trial court apparently based its finding against the district on negligence for withdrawing the qualified teacher from the class, which the court noted, implied the teacher had not returned to the class prior to the accident. The testimony of the teacher and three of the students was contrary however. The Appellate Court concluded the teacher had returned and ruled the trial court in error for holding the school negligent for failing to provide adequate supervision.

The court held that the teacher aide owed no duty to the students once the teacher had returned. The court went on to state that the game being played by the boys was a normal activity for boys this age and was one probably played at home as well. While saying it hesitated to find that the teacher had breached her duty in this case, the court held that it felt bound to consider the testimony of the teacher who said she "considered it her duty to stop rough-housing and that she would have stopped the game had she seen it." Noting the evidence supported the conclusion that the game had gone on for some 10-20 minutes, the court ruled the teacher should have noticed the activity within that time.

The Appellate court held the teacher to be 5 percent negligent. The decision left the plaintiff with a $10,000 judgment. However, the plaintiff was left to pay 95 percent of the trial and Appellate Court costs with the defendant responsible for the remaining 5 percent.

Note. The finding of this court is bizarre at best and certainly should not be relied upon for precedent of any kind. The case does, however, present a couple of important considerations for physical educators and coaches. While some teacher aides hold valid teaching certificates, most do not. Without a valid teaching certificate, they cannot legally assume solo responsibility for classroom instruction. Even where they possess a valid certificate, the regular teacher is the one who has the assigned responsibility for the class and assumes supervisory responsibility over the actions of the aide. Before delegating any responsibility for instruction to an aide, a great deal of communication about activities, progressions, and classroom expectations needs to take place. Second, the appropriateness of an activity needs to be closely scrutinized. What students do at home or away from school in unsupervised situations should not serve as a guide to what is appropriate in an instructional program.

The finding in this case could have been weighted much heavier, if not completely, in favor of the plaintiff. In addition to the legal and prudent use of teacher aides, the court should have been asked to examine the appropriateness of the activity and where it fits into the district curriculum, the lack of safety equipment where tackling occurs, and the adequacy of both the instruction and supervision within the class.

Brahatcek v. Millard School District No. 17
273 N.W. 2d 680

Issue: Inadequate supervision by student teacher — Student
absent on day of safety instruction in golf class

Level of Court: State Supreme Court
Date/State: 1979/Nebraska
Decision: Plaintiff/Affirmed

A 14-year-old boy was fatally injured during a physical education
class when a classmate accidently struck him with a golf club. The
evidence showed that the plaintiff's son was absent on the first day
of the unit when the rules of safety were discussed. Two teachers
were assigned to the combined class of boys and girls, with a total of
57 students enrolled. On the first day, in addition to safety instruction, students were instructed on the golf grip, stance and swing.

One of the regular teachers was absent the day of the accident,
the second day of the unit. His place was taken by a student teacher
who had been at the school for five weeks and had assisted with four
to six golf classes on the previous two days. The regular teacher
present repeated the instructions and divided the class into small
groups to practice the grip and swing.

The plaintiff's son had never swung a golf club and when his turn
came, he asked for help. A classmate volunteered to demonstrate the
proper stance and grip and to demonstrate a few practice swings.
The plaintiff's son moved closer to the boy demonstrating, who was
unaware anyone was standing near him. While observing a swing, the
plaintiff's son was struck in the head by the golf club. The blow
rendered him unconscious and he died two days later without
regaining consciousness.

Testimony showed that on Monday, the first day of instruction,
one person from each group would walk up to their respective mats.
The two regular instructors would see to it that only one individual
was at each mat when the students were to commence their swings.
They would walk back and forth behind the students who were
hitting, offering individual instruction and at the same time making
sure no other students were up and in the way. On Tuesday, the
second day, this procedure was not followed. Testimony indicated
there was a fair amount of milling around by students. After giving

the beginning instructions, the regular teacher focussed her attention on the girls in the class. At the time of the accident, the student teacher was giving individualized instruction to a boy at one of the mats. It was clear from the evidence that general supervision of the entire group was lacking. Expert testimony stressed the importance of having the entire class in view. Given the nature of the activity, expert testimony indicated that a whistle should have been blown and the class stopped if and when it became necessary to give a student individualized instruction. It was argued that had the same procedures used on the first day been followed, students would not have been assisting one another and the risk of harm to the deceased would have been observed. The student teacher testified that he had no lesson plan because the regular teacher was going to handle that. He further stated he gave no oral instructions to any of the students as a whole.

The parents of the deceased based their wrongful death suit against the district on negligent supervision. The defendants claimed that the action of the fellow student was an intervening cause of the accident and that they were thereby relieved of any negligence. In addition, they claimed the deceased was contributorily negligent.

The trial court ruled the district was negligent in its supervision of the golf class and that there was no evidence to support a claim of contributory negligence on the part of the deceased. The court held that the deceased could not have appreciated the danger of the situation as he had never played or become familiar with the sport and had received absolutely no instruction due, in part, to his absence the previous class period. The court held that the district should have been able to foresee the danger that could result from an activity such as this one when dealing with a bunch of inexperienced ninth graders. The court ruled the lack of proper supervision was the proximate cause of the student's death. The Supreme Court upheld the $53,470 in damages awarded by the trial court.

IN SUMMARY

THE REASONABLY PRUDENT PHYSICAL
EDUCATOR OR COACH:

1. Is well informed of all requirements and guidelines relative to the use of practicum students and student teachers which are included in the contract between the university and the cooperating school district.

2. Is well informed of any state statutes regulating the duties and responsibilities which practicum students and student teachers may assume.

3. Provides ongoing and direct supervision to any practicum student or student teacher under his/her control.

4. Adequately assesses and/or evaluates the capabilities, strengths and weaknesses of the practicum or student teacher before allowing them to assume any duties.

5. Provides the student teacher or practicum student with a copy of the district curriculum guide, department and school policy handbooks and a copy of emergency first aid procedures, including appropriate phone numbers.

6. Reviews and approves all unit plans as well as all daily written lesson plans.

7. Retains control over the class or team.

SUBSTITUTE TEACHERS

School board policy as well as professional practice suggest that teachers have a duty to provide substitute teachers with adequate and complete lesson plans when they are absent from duty whether for illness, professional activities or personal leave. The purpose of these plans is to allow the orderly continuance of the educational process. In the physical education setting, this means not only continuance of the unit but the safe and proper conducting of the activities themselves.

While substitute teachers will clearly be held liable for their own negligent acts, some case law exists which suggests that the absent teacher might also be held accountable for injuries which occur in their classrooms while under the charge of a substitute. A key element in negligence is foreseeability. Teachers owe a duty of reasonable and ordinary care under the circumstances any time a foreseeable risk of harm exists. Substitutes entering a classroom are at a distinct disadvantage in that they have little or no knowledge of the class or the students in that class prior to their actual arrival. Their lack of knowledge and understanding can, in many circumstances, put them in a situation where they are unable to foresee risks which would be easily foreseeable by the regular teacher. This is a situation which can be easily remedied by a complete and detailed lesson plan.

In Larson v. Independent School District, 289 N.W. 2d 112 (1980), previously discussed in the section on supervision (page 24), a student suffered paralyzing injuries in a gymnastics class which had been taken over just nine days earlier by a new teacher. The court requested the defendant to supply the lesson plans in order to show the teaching progressions employed. If a student were injured in a gymnastics class being taught by a substitute, there is no reason to believe that the progression of skills employed prior to the injury would not still be at issue. It is important that lesson plans left for substitutes properly fit into and address the issue of skill progressions. The lesson plan should adequately outline the skills to be taught, the rules to be employed, the drills to be used and the safety instructions to be given. In short, the lesson plan should sufficiently detail the lesson to be carried out.

In another case previously discussed in this section (page 186), Brahatcek v. Millard School District, 273 N.W. 2d 680 (1979), a point was made during trial of the fact that a student teacher who substituted for a regular teacher on the second day of a golf unit, did not have a lesson plan nor did he receive any instructions from either the absent teacher or the other teacher about the class activity. As a result of negligent supervision, a young man died from injuries received in the class. Substitutes should not be left in charge without supplying them with a lesson plan.

In yet another previously discussed case in the supervision section, Cook v. Bennett, 288 N.W. 609 (1979) (page 68), an absent teacher was named as a defendant along with the principal in an action to recover damages for injuries received in the game "kill" during recess. Evidence indicated that the game, which included group tackling, was played on numerous previous occasions with the apparent approval of both the teacher and principal. The court found the game to be ultrahazardous and held the principal negligent for his supervision of both staff and students. While the absent teacher was not held negligent in this case, the case nonetheless shows a willingness on the part of plaintiffs to hold absent teachers accountable for injuries which occur during their absence and for which they are perceived to play a contributing role.

In both Summers v. Milwaukie Union School District, 481 P. 2d 369 (1971) (page 72) and Luce v. Board of Education, 157 N.Y.S. 2d 123 (1956), the issue was one of the prior condition of students. The students in these cases received injuries while participating in activities which they were either excused from by doctor permission or should have been exempted from due to medical conditions or prior injury. The duty of physical educators and coaches to be aware of the health status of students under their charge is clear. Again, in the absence of a lesson plan alerting them to such circumstances and conditions, the substitute is in no position to adequately foresee the risks posed by activity to students who should legitimately be precluded from participating for one reason or another.

Awareness of special discipline problems is also needed by substitutes who are expected to maintain an orderly and safe instructional environment in the absence of the regular teacher. Lack of awareness was at issue in the case of Ferraro v. Board of Education of the City of New York, 212 N.Y.S. 2d 615 (1961). In this case a student was injured after being assaulted by another student in a class which was overseen by a substitute teacher. Evidence at trial indicated that the attacking student had been transferred from another school earlier in the year because of discipline problems and had been a chronic behavior problem since enrolling. While the classroom teacher was not a defendant in this case, the court held the principal liable. Testimony established that the substitute had received no information relative to the disruptive student prior to assuming her duties. In holding the principal liable, the court stated that "It is clear that the assault itself cannot be the basis for liability of the defendant. It is the failure of the principal to have alerted the substitute, thereby depriving her of the opportunity of using her own judgment, which I believe constitutes the negligence in this case. Had she been told, she would have been in a position to decide whether anything further was required to reasonably be done to avoid the trouble."

Much of the needed information referred to above can be printed up and filed so that it can be easily attached to the daily activity plan when absence by the regular teacher is required. Only through a complete and detailed lesson plan can the substitute be in a position to adequately foresee many of the risks which confront group activity

IN SUMMARY

THE REASONABLY PRUDENT PHYSICAL EDUCATOR OR COACH:

1. Provides a detailed lesson plan for use by the substitute teacher, including safety precautions.

2. Alerts the substitute teacher to any student who is precluded from full participation due to illness or injury.

3. Alerts the substitute teacher to chronically disruptive or physically aggressive students.

4. Alerts the substitute to any known hazardous conditions within the facilities or grounds.

5. Avoids having unknown substitutes carry on any activities which contain an elevated risk of injury.

6. Provides the substitute with the names of a couple of nearby staff who can assist in an emergency.

Glossary of Terms

All definitions are taken from the 6th edition of *Black's Law Dictionary* (West Publishing Co., St. Paul, MN, 1990).

Abrogate: To annul, revoke, cancel, repeal, or destroy. To annul or repeal an order or rule issued by a subordinate authority; to repeal a former law by legislative act, or by usage.

Assumption of Risk: The doctrine of assumption of risk, also known as volenti non fit injuria, means legally that a plaintiff may not recover from an injury to which he assents, i.e., that a person may not recover for an injury received when he voluntarily exposes himself to a known and appreciated danger.

Attractive Nuisance: The doctrine is that person who has an instrumentality, agency, or condition upon his own premises, or who creates such condition on the premises of another or in a public place, which may reasonably be apprehended to be a source of danger to children, is under a duty to take such precautions as a reasonably prudent man would take to prevent injury to children of tender years who he knows to be accustomed to resort there, or who may, by reason of something there which may be expected to attract them, come there to play.

Battery: Intentional and wrongful physical contact with a person without his or her consent that entails some injury or offensive touching. Criminal battery, defined as the unlawful application of force to the person of another.

Breach of Duty: In a general sense, any violation or omission of a legal or moral duty. More particularly, the neglect or failure to fulfill in a just and proper manner the duties of an office or fiduciary employment.

Burden of Proof: In the law of evidence, the necessity or duty of affirmatively proving a fact or facts in a dispute on an issue raised between the parties in a cause.

Common Law: As distinguished from statutory law created by the enactment of legislatures, the common law comprises the body of those principles and rules of action, relating to the government and security of persons and property, which derive their authority solely from usages and customs of immemorial antiquity, or from the judgments and decrees of the courts recognizing, affirming, and enforcing such usages and customs.

Comparative Negligence: Under comparative negligence statutes or doctrines, negligence is measured in terms of percentage, and any damages allowed shall be diminished in proportion to amount of negligence attributable to the person for whose injury, damage or death recovery is sought.

Compensatory Damages: Compensatory damages are such as will compensate the injured party for the injury sustained, and nothing more; actual damages.

Concurring Opinion: A separate opinion delivered by one or more judges which agrees with the decision of the majority of the court but offering own reasons for reaching that decision.

Contributory Negligence: The act or omission amounting to want of ordinary care on part of complaining party, which, concurring with defendant's negligence, is proximate cause of injury.

Damages: A pecuniary compensation or indemnity which may be recovered in the courts by any person who has suffered loss, detriment, or injury, whether to his person, property, or rights through the unlawful act or omission or negligence of another. A sum of money awarded to a person injured by the tort of another.

Declatory Judgment: Statutory remedy for the determination of a justiciable controversy where the plaintiff is in doubt as to his legal rights. A binding adjudication of the rights and status of litigants even though no consequential relief is awarded.

Defendant: The person defending or denying; the party against whom relief or recovery is sought in an action or suit or the accused in a criminal case.

Demurrer: An allegation of a defendant, which, admitting the matters of fact alleged by the complaint to be true, shows that as they are therein set forth they are insufficient for the plaintiff to proceed upon or to oblige the defendant to answer; the formal mode of disputing the sufficiency in law of the pleading of the other side.

Deposition: The testimony of a witness taken upon oral question or written interrogatories, not in open court, but in pursuance of a commission to take testimony issued by a court, or under a general law or court rule on the subject, and reduced to writing and duly authenticated, and intended to be used in preparation and upon the trial of a civil action or criminal prosecution.

Directed Verdict: In a case in which the party with the burden of proof has failed to present a prima facie case for jury consideration, the trial judge may order the entry of a verdict without allowing the jury to consider it, because, as a matter of law, there can be only one such verdict.

Discretionary Act: Those acts wherein there is no hard and fast rule as to course of conduct that one must or must not take and, if there is clearly defined rule, such would eliminate discretion. One which requires exercise in judgment and choice and involves what is just and proper under the circumstances.

Dissenting Opinion: The term is most commonly used to denote the explicit disagreement of one or more judges of a court with the decision passed by the majority upon a case before them.

Duty: In negligence case term may be defined as obligation, to which law will give recognition and effect, to comport to a particular standard of conduct toward another, and the duty is invariably the same, one must conform to legal standard of reasonable conduct in the light of apparent risk.

Exculpatory Clause: A contract clause which releases one of the parties from liability for his or her wrongful acts.

Expert Witness: One who by reason of education or specialized experience possesses superior knowledge respecting a subject about which persons having no particular training are incapable of forming an accurate opinion or deducing correct conclusions.

Foreseeability: The ability to see or know in advance; e.g., the reasonable anticipation that harm or injury is a likely result from certain acts or omissions.

Governmental Function: The functions of a municipality which are essential to its existence.

Governmental Immunity: The federal, state, and local governments are not amendable to actions in tort except in cases in which they have consented to be sued.

Gross Negligence: The intentional failure to perform a manifest duty in reckless disregard of the consequences as affecting the life or property of another.

Hold Harmless: A contractual arrangement whereby one party assumes the liability inherent in a situation, thereby relieving the other party of responsibility.

Implied Warranty: A promise arising by operation of law, that something which is sold shall be merchantable and fit for the purpose for which the seller has reason to know that it is required.

Indemnify: To save harmless; to secure against loss or damage; to give security for the reimbursement of a person in case of an anticipated loss falling upon him.

Injunction: A judicial process operating in personam, and requiring person to whom it is directed to do or refrain from doing a particular thing.

In Loco Parentis: In the place of a parent; instead of a parent; charged, factitiously, with a parent's rights, duties and responsibilities.

Intervening Cause: In tort law, as will relieve of liability for an injury, is an independent cause which intervenes between the original wrongful act or omission and the injury, turns aside the natural sequence of events, and produces a result which would not otherwise have followed and which could not have been reasonably anticipated.

Invitee: A person is an "invitee" on land of another if (1) he enters by invitation, express or implied, (2) his entry is connected with the owner's business or with an activity the owner conducts or permits to be conducted on his land and (3) there is mutuality of benefit or benefit to the owner.

Joint Tortfeasors: Term refers to two or more persons jointly or severally liable in tort for the same injury to person or property.

Judgment: The official and authentic decision of a court of justice upon the respective rights and claims of the parties to an action or suit therein litigated and submitted to its determination.

Judgment Notwithstanding the Decision: A judgment entered by order of court for the plaintiff (or defendant) although there has been a verdict for the defendant (or plaintiff)... A judgment in favor of one party notwithstanding the finding of a verdict in favor of the other party.

Jurisdiction: Areas of authority; the geographic area in which a court has power or types of cases it has power to hear.

Leave of Court: Permission obtained from a court to take some action which, without such permission, would not be allowable; as, to receive an extension of time to answer a complaint.

Liable: Bound or obliged in law or equity; responsible; chargeable; answerable; compellable to make satisfaction, compensation, or restitution.

Litigation: Legal action, including all proceedings therein. Contest in a court of law for the purpose of enforcing a right or seeking a remedy.

Malfeasance: The commission of some act which is positively unlawful.

Ministerial Act: One which a person or board performs under a given state of facts in a prescribed manner in obedience to the mandate of legal authority without regard to or the exercise of his or their own judgment upon the propriety of the act being done.

Ministerial Duty: One regarding which nothing is left to discretion. A simple and definite duty, imposed by law, and arising under conditions admitted or proved to exist.

Misfeasance: The improper performance of some act which a person may lawfully do.

Negligence: The failure to use such care as a reasonably prudent and careful person would use under similar circumstances; it is the doing of some act which a person of ordinary prudence would not have done under similar circumstances or failure to do what a person of ordinary prudence would have done under similar circumstances.

Nonfeasance: Nonperformance of some act which person is obligated or has responsibility to perform; omission to perform a required duty at all, or total neglect of duty.

Plaintiff: A person who brings an action . . . a person who seeks remedial relief for an injury to rights.

Precedent: An adjudged case or decision of a court, considered as furnishing an example or authority for an identical or similar case afterwards arising or a similar question of law.

Preponderance of Evidence: Evidence which is of greater weight or more convincing than the evidence which is offered in opposition to it; that is, evidence which as a whole, shows that the fact sought to be proved is more probable than not.

Prima Facie: A fact presumed to be true unless disproved by some evidence to the contrary.

Proximate Cause: That which, in a natural and continuous sequence, unbroken by an efficient intervening cause, produces injury, and without which the result would not have occurred.

Prudence: Carefulness, precaution, attentiveness, and good judgment, as applied to action or conduct.

Punitive Damages: Damages on an increased scale, awarded to the plaintiff over and above what will barely compensate him for his property loss, where the wrong done to him was aggravated by circumstances of violence, oppression, malice, fraud, or wanton and wicked conduct on the part of the defendant, and are intended to solace the plaintiff for mental anguish, laceration of feelings, shame, degradation, or other aggravations of the original wrong, or else to punish the defendant for his evil behavior or to make an example of him.

Question of Fact: An issue involving the resolution of a factual dispute and hence, within the province of the jury in contrast to a question of law.

Question of Law: An issue which involves the application or interpretation of a law and hence, within the province of the judge and not the jury.

Reasonable: Fair, proper, just, moderate, suitable under the circumstances.

Remand: To send back. The act of an appellate court when it sends a case back to the same trial court and orders the trial court to conduct limited new hearings or an entirely new trial, or to take some further action.

Res Ipsa Loquitas: The thing speaks for itself. Rebuttable presumption or inference that defendant was negligent, which arises upon proof that instrumentality causing injury was in defendant's exclusive control, and that the accident was one which ordinarily does not happen in the absence of negligence.

Respondeat Superior: Let the master answer. This doctrine or maxim means that a master is liable in certain cases for the wrongful acts of his servant and a principal for those of his agent. Under this doctrine master is responsible for want of care on servant's part toward those to whom master owes duty to use care, provided failure of servant to use such care occurred in course of his employment.

Save Harmless: A provision in a document by which one party agrees to indemnify and hold harmless another party as to claims and suits which may be asserted against him.

Scope of Employment: An employee acts in scope of his employment, for the purpose of invoking a doctrine of respondeat superior, when he is doing something in furtherance of duties he owes to his employer and where employer is, or could be, exercising some control, directly or indirectly, over employee's activities.

Set Aside: To reverse, vacate, cancel, annul, or revoke a judgment, order, etc.

Standard of Care: In law of negligence, that degree of care which a reasonably prudent person should exercise in same or similar circumstances.

Strict Liability: A concept applied by the courts in product liability cases in which the seller is liable for any and all defective or hazardous products which unduly threaten a consumer's personal safety.

Substantive Due Process: Such may be broadly defined as the constitutional guarantee that no person shall be arbitrarily deprived of his life, liberty, or property. The essence of substantive due process is protection from arbitrary and unreasonable action.

Summary Judgment: Procedural device available for prompt and expeditious disposition of controversy without trial when there is no dispute as to either material fact, or inferences to be drawn from undisputed facts, or if only question of law is involved. Federal Rule of Civil Procedure 56 permits any party to a civil action to move for a summary judgment on a claim, counterclaim or cross-claim when he believes that there is no genuine issue of material fact and that he is entitled to prevail as a matter of law.

Tort: A private or civil wrong or injury, including action for bad faith breach of contract, for which the court will provide a remedy in the form of an action for damages.

Ultra Vires Act: An act performed without any authority to act on subject. Acts beyond the scope of the powers of a corporation, as defined by its charter or laws of state of incorporation.

Vacate: To annul; to set aside; to cancel or rescind. To render an act void.

Waiver: The renunciation, repudiation, abandonment, or surrender of some claim, right, privilege, or of the opportunity to take advantage of some defect, irregularity, or wrong.

Willful and Wanton Misconduct: Conduct which is committed with an intentional or reckless disregard for the safety of others or with an intentional disregard of a duty necessary to the safety of another's property. . . Conduct which is intentional or committed under circumstances exhibiting a reckless disregard for the safety of others, such as failure, after knowledge of an impending danger, to exercise ordinary care to prevent it or a failure to discover the dangers through recklessness or carelessness when it could have been discovered by the exercise of ordinary care.

Additional Cases of Interest

Instruction and Teaching Methodology

Dibortolo v. Metropolitan School District of Washington Township, 440 N.E. 2d 506 (Improper instruction of vertical jump test)

Weiss v. Collinsville Community School District No. 10, 456 N.E. 2d 614 (Improper instruction — failure to instruct about sliding in softball)

Berg v. Merricks, 318 A. 2d 220 (Teaching methodology — back pullover on trampoline)

Baird v. Hosmer, 347 N.E. 2d 533 (Improper instruction, inappropriate vaulting equipment, and lack of landing mats)

Lovitt v. Concord School District, 228 N.W. 2d 479 (Strenuous workout leads to heat prostration)

Montague v. School Board of the Thornton Fractional Township North High School District, 373 N.E. 2d 719 (Improper use of spotters in gymnastics)

Vargo v. Svitchan, 301 N.W. 2d 1 (Preseason weight training for football — coercion)

Cherney v. Board of Education of the School District of the City of White Plains, 297 N.Y.S. 2d 668 (Improper instruction — student expressed apprehension about the activity)

Buckvar v. Syosset Central School District, 538 N.Y.S. 2d 563 (Lack of safety precautions in flag football)

Supervision

Ragnone v. Portland School District 1J, 633 P. 2d 1287 (Improper supervision — teacher absent from class)

Holsapple v. Casey Community Unit School District C1, 510 N.E. 2d 499 (Locker room unsupervised and lack of spring loaded or pneumatic device on door)

Hyman v. Green, 403 N.W. 2d 597 (Failure to carry out supervisory duty in physical education class)

Chilton v. Cook County School District No. 207, 347 N.E. 2d 705 (Inadequate supervision of trampoline activity)

Grant v. Lake Oswego School District No. 7, 515 P. 2d 947 (Inadequate supervision for use of springboard)

Poelker v. Macon County Union School District No. 5, 571 N.E. 2d 479 (Lack of adequate supervision of discus throw during track meet)

Merkley v. Palmyra-Macedon Central School District, 515 N.Y.S. 2d 932 (Improper supervision for shot put)

Cepelina v. South Milwaukie School Board, 243 N.W. 2d 183 (Negligent supervision — student hit by softball bat)

Hauser v. South Orangetown Central School District No. 1, 376 N.Y.S. 2d 608 (Failure to keep activity within the ability of students in high jump)

Ward v. Newfield Central School District No. 1, 412 N.Y.S. 2d 57 (Inadequate supervision — failure to enforce safety rules)

Stephens v. Shelbyville Central Schools, 318 N.E. 2d 590 (Prior physical condition of student)

Sitomer v. Half Hollow Hills Central School District, 520 N.Y.S. 2d 37 (Lack of physical maturity required for athletic program)

Swiderski v. Board of Education-City School District of Albany, 408 N.Y.S. 2d 744 (Precluding participation in athletics due to defective vision in one eye)

Rollins v. Concordia Parish School Board, 465 So. 2d 213 (Not attending to a dangerous situation)

James v. Cloversville Enlarged School District, 548 N.Y.S. 2d 87 (Ignoring previous complaints of harassment)

Kingsley v. Independent School District No. 2, 251 N.W. 2d 634 (Failure to take corrective measures in maintaining school discipline)

Thomas v. Cascade Union High School District No. 5, 724 P. 2d 330 (Physical educator dismissed for kicking student)

Hogenson v. Williams, 542 S.W. 2d 456 (Physical abuse — football coach strikes player's helmet and pulls on face mask)

Frank v. Orleans Parish School Board, 195 So. 2d 451 (Excessive force in discipline)

Cook v. School District UH3J, 731 P. 2d 443 (Lack of supervision at high school basketball game)

Kluka v. Livingston Parish School Board, 433 So. 2d 302 (Coach wrestling athlete)

Equipment, Grounds, Facilities

Stanley v. Board of Education of City of Chicago, 293 N.E. 2d 417 (Unsafe equipment — untaped bat)

Gerrity v. Beatty, 373 N.E. 2d 1323 (Ill-fitted football helmet)

Everet v. Bucky Warren, Inc., 380 N.E. 2d 653 (School supplies unsafe helmet to hockey player)

Hornyak v. Pomfret School, 783 F. 2d 284 (Harvard step test bench on uneven ground)

Bowers v. DuPage County Regional Board of School Trustees Distrct No. 4, 539 N.E. 2d 246 (Willful and wanton misconduct — improper supervision and equipment, rope ladder)

Bouillon v. Harry Gill Company and Litchfield Public School District No. 12, 301 N.E. 2d 627 (Pole vault standards improperly constructed and located)

Siau v. Rapides Parish School Board, 264 So. 2d 372 (Student impaled by javelin left sticking in ground)

Singer v. School District of Philadelphia, 513 A. 2d 1108 (Mats around vaulting horse, involving real property exception to governmental immunity)

McClosky v. Abington School District, 539 A. 2d 946 (Fall from gymnastics rings, involving real estate exception to governmental immunity)

Fallon v. Indian Trail School, 500 N.E. 2d 101 (Hazardous equipment — trampoline)

Moschella v. Archdiocese of New York, 383 N.Y.S. 2d 49 (Failure to supply softball face mask)

Rutter v. Northeastern Beaver County School District, 437 A. 2d 1198 (No protective gear for jungle football during summer practice)

Lynch v. Board of Education of Collinsville Community Unit District No. 10, 412 N.E. 2d 447 (Lack of protective equipment in powderpuff football)

Thomas v. Chicago Board of Education, 395 N.E. 2d 538 (Coach fails to inspect football equipment)

Fusilier v. Northbrook Excess and Surplus Insurance Company, 471 So. 2d 761 (Dangerous grounds — broken chain link fence in tall uncut grass)

Ardoin v. Evangeline Parish School Board, 376 So. 2d 372 (Unsafe maintenance of grounds — concrete slab in playing area)

Overcash v. Statesville City Board of Education, 348 S.E. 2d 524 (Spike imbedded in ground along first base line)

Lejeune v. Acadia Parish School Board, 517 So. 2d 1030 (Dangerous grounds — cable barrier between parking lot and playing area)

McInnis v. Town of Tewksbury, 473 N.E. 2d 1160 (Unsafe grounds — inadequate sand in long jump pit)

Clary v. Alexander Board of Education, 212 S.E. 2d 160 (Unsafe facilities — glass panel close to court boundary)

Gump v. Chartiers-Houston School District, 558 A. 2d 589 (Defective facility — lack of safety glass)

Thomas v. St. Mary's Roman Catholic Church, 283 N.W. 2d 254 (Defective facilities — glass panels adjacent to gym entry way)

Prest v. Sparta Community Unit School District, 510 N.E. 2d 595 (Dangerous facilities — unprotected concrete riser in gymnasium)

Tijerina v. Evans, 501 N.E. 2d 995 (Open bleachers during indoor whiffleball game)

Administration of First Aid

Bernesak v. Catholic Bishop of Chicago, 409 N.E. 2d 287 (Improper care of injured and allowing dangerous game to be played)

Endnotes

1. Neil J. Dougherty, *Principles of Safety in Physical Education and Sport* (Reston: American Alliance for Health, Physical Education, Recreation and Dance, 1987), 3.
2. William L. Prosser and W. Page Keeton, *Law of Torts*, 5thed. (St. Paul: West, 1984), 5.
3. W. Page Keeton and Robert F. Keeton, *Torts: Cases and Materials*, 2nd ed. (St. Paul: West, 1977), 2.
4. Betty van der Smissen, *Legal Liability and Risk Management for Public and Private Entities*, Vol. I. (Cincinnati: Anderson, 1990), chapter 1, 67.
5. Clarence Morris and Robert C. Morris, Jr. *Morris on Tort.* (Mineola, New York: Foundation Press, 1980), 57.
6. Henry Campbell Black, *Black's Law Dictionary*, 6th ed. (St. Paul: West, 1990), 1103, 736.
7. van der Smissen, chapter 2, 60.
8. van der Smissen, chapter 3, 78.
9. van der Smissen, chapter 3, 108.
10. Wesley H. Winborne, Ed., *Civil Actions Against State Government* (Colorado Springs: Shepard's/McGraw-Hill, 1982), 20.
11. American Law Institute, *Restatement of Torts* (Philadelphia, 1972), s 463.
12. Prosser and Keeton, 451.
13. van der Smissen, chapter 5, 235.
14. William P. Statsky, *Torts: Personal Injury Litigation* (St. Paul: West, 1982), 400.
15. Boyd B. Baker, *Physical Education and the Law: A Proposed Course for the Professional Preparation of Physical Educators* (Diss. University of Oregon, 1970), 34.
16. Prosser and Keeton, 398.
17. Black.

References

Books

Appenzeller, Herb. *Athletics and the Law*. Charlottesville, VA: Michie, 1975.

Appenzeller, Herb. *Physical Education and the Law*. Charlottesville, VA: Michie, 1978.

Appenzeller, Herb, and Thomas Appenzeller. *Sports and the Courts*. Charlottesville, VA: Michie, 1980.

Appenzeller, Herb, et al. *Sports and Law*. St. Paul: West, 1984.

Appenzeller, Herb. *The Right to Participate*. Charlottesville, VA: Michie, 1983.

Arnold, Don E. *Legal Considerations in the Administration of Public School Physical Education and Athletic Programs*. Springfield: Thomas, 1983.

Baley, James A. and David L. Matthews. *Law and Liability in Athletics, Physical Education, and Recreation*. Boston: Allyn and Bacon, 1984.

Clement, Annie. *Law in Sport and Physical Activity*. Indianapolis: Benchmark, 1988.

Dougherty, Neil J., ed. *Principles of Safety in Physical Education and Sport*. Reston, VA: American Alliance for Health, Physical Education, Recreation and Dance, 1987.

Drowatsky, John N. *Legal Issues in Sport and Physical Education Management*. Champaign, IL: Stipes, 1984.

Jefferies, Stephen C, Director, Level 2, American Coaching Effectiveness Program. *Sport Law Study Guide*. Champaign, IL: Human Kinetics, 1985.

Keeton, W. Page, Dan B. Dobbs, Robert F. Keeton, and David G. Owen. *Prosser and Keeton on Torts*. St. Paul: West, 1984.

Keeton, Page, and Robert F. Keeton. *Torts: Cases and Materials*. St. Paul: West, 1971.

LaMorte, Michael W. *School Law: Cases and Concepts*. Englewood Cliffs, NJ: Prentice Hall, 1982.

Morris, Clarence and C. Robert Morris, Jr. *Morris on Torts*. Mineola, NY: Foundation Press, 1980.

National Association for Sport and Physical Education (NASPE). *Current Issues in Sport Law*. Reston, VA: American Alliance for Health, Physical Education, Recreation and Dance, 1987.

.ganization on Legal Problems of Education (NOLPE). *The Yearbook* *School Law*. Topeka, KS: 1973 to present (an annual publication).

.ard, Gary. *Law for Physical Educators and Coaches*. Columbus, OH: Horizons, 1989.

Nygaard, Gary, and Thomas H. Boone. *Coaches Guide to Sport Law*. Champaign, Illinois: Human Kinetics, 1985.

Oregon Department of Education. *Legal Liability in the Gymnasium*. Salem, OR, 1988.

Prosser, William L. , and W. Page Keeton. *Law of Torts*. 5th ed. St. Paul: West, 1984.

Riffer, Jeffery K. *Sports and Recreational Injuries*. Colorado Springs: Shepard's McGraw-Hill, 1985.

Statsky, William P. *Torts: Personal Injury Litigation*. St. Paul: West, 1982.

van der Smissen, Betty. *Legal Liability and Risk Management for Public and Private Entities*, Vol. I-III. Cincinnati, OH: Anderson, 1990.

Periodicals

Education Law Reporter. West Publishing: St. Paul, MN (bi-weekly).

Journal of Legal Aspects of Sport. Society for the Study of Legal Aspects of Sport and Physical Activity, Baylor University (semi-annually)

Journal of Physical Education, Recreation and Dance. American Alliance of Health, Physical Education, Recreation and Dance. Reston, VA (nine issues per year).

Strategies (Courtside Column). American Alliance of Health, Physical Education, Recreation and Dance. Reston, VA (six issues per year).

Law Related Newsletters

From the Gym to the Jury. Center for Sports Law and Risk Management, Dallas, TX (six issues per year)

Sports and the Courts. Winston-Salem, NC (five issues per year)

School Law Reporter. NOLPE, Topeka, KS (monthly)

Legal References

American Jurisprudence. Rochester: Lawyer's Cooperative, 1943 - date.

American Law Reports Annotated. Rochester: Lawyer's Cooperative, 1913 - date.

Atlantic Reporter. St. Paul: West, 1885 - date.

Black, Henry Campbell. *Black's Law Dictionary*. 6th ed. St. Paul: West, 199█

Code of Federal Regulations. Vol. 34. Washington, DC: U.S. Government█
Printing Office, 1986.

Corpus Juris Secundum. New York: American Law Book, 1952 - date.

Eighth Decennial Digest. St. Paul: West, 1978.

Federal Reporter. St. Paul: West, 1880 - date.

Martindale-Hubbel Law Directory. 7 Vols. Summit, New Jersey: Martindale-
Hubbel, Inc. 1987. Vol. 7.

New York Supplement. St. Paul: West, 1888 - date

Ninth Decennial Digest. St. Paul: West, 1983.

North Eastern Reporter. St. Paul: West, 1885 - date.

North Western Reporter. St. Paul: West, 1879 - date.

Pacific Reporter. St. Paul: West, 1887 - date.

Shepard's Citations. Colorado Springs: Shepard's/McGraw-Hill, to date.

South Western Reporter. St. Paul: West, 1886 - date.

Southern Reporter. St. Paul: West, 1886 - date.

West's General Digest. 6th Series. St. Paul: West, 1982-86.

West's General Digest. 7th Series. St. Paul: West, 1986-87.